Simply With Taste

Recipes Compiled by
Carolyn Miller and Ruth Stoltzfus
Illustrated by
Ruth Stoltzfus

Simply with Taste
ISBN 0-9702865-0-3

Cover design by Teresa Hochstetler
Cover artwork by Ruth Stoltzfus

Printed by Carlisle Printing, 2727 TR 421, Sugarcreek, OH 44681

© August 2000 In Pleasant Company

28938 River Road
Millington, MD 21651
410-810-3163

In Pleasant Company

To our friends...

For a number of years, we as a family have tossed around the idea of compiling our recipes. It seemed that we often were making long distance phone calls with questions like, "how do you make this", or "can I have your recipe for...", etc. Now that we have all left home and started our own homes, we look back with fond memories of Mom's tasty cooking and her love of setting a nice table. Cooking is such an essential part of all of our lives and Mom taught us that it's worth doing well.

As you page through this book, you will find many different types and styles of recipes, many reflecting the different areas that we have all lived as well as our Amish/Mennonite heritage. Dad and Mom started their lives together in Northern Indiana in the year of 1953. They made their home there in a close knit Amish community until 1968 when they packed their belongings and moved to Blackville, SC. For fourteen years this was home and living there gave Mom many opportunities to host and cook for Northern family and friends who were traveling through to vacation in the warmer climates of Florida. Dad started his own construction business there but later went into full-time work with Choice Books. This work eventually moved us further South to Jesup, Georgia where they still reside and are the owners of Sugar n' Spice Bake Shop.

As we discussed this book and the recipes that we would include, we soon realized that a lot of our favorite recipes came from our friends and extended families, who have influenced our lives over the years. We thank each one of you who have so generously shared your lives, friendships and last but not least, your recipes.

As with any recipes, these are not ours exclusively, please feel free to share them, adapt them, and claim them for your own! We all adapt our own recipes, adding a dash of 'this' and a taste of 'that' to suit each individual meal or snack. We hope that you will find hours of cooking enjoyment within these pages.

Carolyn
&
Ruth

Do not forget to entertain
strangers, for by so doing
some people have entertained
angels without knowing it.
Hebrews 13:2 NIV

Acknowledgments

Our heartfelt thanks to our husbands, Jason and
Jonas, as well as Michael and Bethany who not only
put up with our long hours, trips away from home,
and our frustrations, but have been the support
system that we needed to keep the book going.

To our proofreaders, Carol Burkholder and Anne
Miller, we thank you for your willingness to work
with our schedules and the time you spent reading
the pages and making needed corrections.

Most of all we are grateful to the One who gave us
life, strength, ability and inspiration.
Our help cometh from the Lord. Ps. 121:2a

Table of Contents

Cheerfully share your home with those who need a meal or a place to stay.
-1 Peter 4:9 NLT

Appetizers,
Snacks,
and
Beverages

APPETIZERS, SNACKS AND BEVERAGES

Country Lemonade

5 lemons
5 limes
5 oranges
3 quarts water
2 cups sugar

Squeeze the juice from four each of the lemons, limes, and oranges. Pour into a gallon container. Add water and sugar to the citrus juice and stir until sugar dissolves. Chill. Thinly slice the remaining fruit and set aside for garnish. (Leave slices whole to place in pitcher or make one cut halfway through to place on the rim of each serving glass.) Serve on ice.

Serves 12 - 16, about 1 gallon.

-Marti

Lemonade Shakes

16 oz. crushed ice
1 cup water
2 1/2 Tbsp. sugar
1/2 lemon

Place the crushed ice in a container that can be sealed, add the water and sugar. Squeeze the lemon, discarding the seeds. Add the juice and the lemon rind. Shake well and serve immediately.

Serves 1.

-Krystal

Party Punch

2 cups sugar
6 cups water

In saucepan, heat water and sugar until sugar is dissolved. Set aside and cool.

1 can (46 oz.) orange juice
1 can (46 oz.) pineapple juice
6 ripe bananas, mashed
2 Tbsp. lemon juice

Add these ingredients to the cooled sugar water, and stir until well mixed. Freeze.

1 liter ginger ale

Remove the punch from the freezer 1 hour before serving, add the ginger ale and serve slightly slushy.

This is a cool and refreshing drink to serve at any special occasion party in the summertime... it's easy to prepare and can be made the day before the event.

-Mom

4

Sparkling Grape Juice

2 (12 oz.) cans frozen or canned
   grape juice concentrate
4 cups water
2/3 cup lemon juice
1 (12 oz.) can frozen orange juice
   concentrate, thawed
1 1/2 cup sugar

*Mix all ingredients in a one gallon
container. Chill.
(Option for a cool summer drink,
place in freezer until chilled and
slightly slushy, about 2 - 3 hours.)*

1 - 2 liter bottle ginger ale

*Add the ginger ale and serve
immediately.*

Makes approximately 1 1/2
gallons.

-Carolyn

Orange Refresher

1 (6 oz.) can frozen orange juice
   concentrate, thawed
1/3 cup sugar
1/3 cup nonfat dry milk powder
1 1/2 tsp. vanilla extract
3/4 cup cold water

*Combine the orange juice, sugar,
milk powder, vanilla, and cold
water in a blender and process at
high speed.*

12 ice cubes
orange slices
fresh mint sprigs

*Add the ice cubes, a few at a time.
Blend until slushy. Garnish with
orange slices and mint, and serve
immediately.*

Serves 4

-Marti

Strawberry Slush

You'll need about 5 ice cube trays to freeze this beverage. If you don't have that many, fill the ones you have; freeze and place the frozen cubes in a bag and continue to freeze the remaining base.

1 (20 oz.) pkg. fresh or frozen
    strawberries, thawed
2 (15 1/4 oz.) cans crushed
    pineapple
3 cups orange juice

lemon-lime carbonated
    beverage, chilled

In blender, combine one half of the strawberries, 1 can of undrained pineapple, and half of the orange juice. Blend until smooth.

Pour the mixture into ice cube trays.

Repeat with the remaining half of the ingredients.

Cover and freeze until solid.

At serving time place the cubes into a large ice bucket, or bowl.
To serve place 2 or 3 cubes into each glass and slowly pour carbonated beverage over the cubes. Stir to make a slush.

Serves 30.

~Ruth

Fruit Dip

8 oz. cream cheese, softened
1 (7 oz.) jar marshmallow creme

Whip the cream cheese and marshmallow creme together until light and fluffy.

1 tsp. rum extract

Add the rum extract and blend.

Optional; add a few drops of red food coloring for an attractive pink color.

Chill until ready to serve.

Fruit Ideas and Tips

cantaloupe
kiwi
grapes
strawberries
pineapple
bananas
apples
plums
pears

To keep the fruit from browning, dip into pineapple or lemon juice and let set for about 4 - 5 min.

It is a good idea to wait to slice the bananas till right before serving time.

Keep your strawberries whole with the tops still attached for a "pick-up" handle.

Serving ideas;
*Use a vegetable dip tray and place fresh fruits around the dip bowl.
*Make a 'fruit cascade' and serve the dip alongside of the fruit.
*Place the dip in individual cups to be easily picked up on a buffet line.

~Ruth

Taco Dip

2 - 16 oz. cans refried beans
2 cups salsa, medium
1 tsp. red hot pepper sauce
1/2 tsp. chili powder

Mix these ingredients with an electric mixer on low speed until well blended. Spread evenly into a jelly-roll pan (14"x11"x1-1/2").

1 cup salad dressing
2 cups sour cream
1 (1 1/4 oz.) packet taco
    seasoning mix

Combine the next 3 ingredients and spread evenly over the bean mixture.

3 cups shredded lettuce
1 cup diced tomato
1/2 cup chopped onion
1/2 cup chopped green or red
    pepper, or 1/4 cup each

Sprinkle the vegetables evenly over the top, (all vegetables are optional and can be increased or decreased to taste).

2 cups shredded cheddar cheese
Nacho chips

Top with the cheese and serve with nacho chips

-carolyn

Salsa Dip

8 oz. cream cheese, softened
1 1/2 cups cheddar cheese, shredded
1/2 cup sour cream
1/2 cup salsa, medium or hot, to taste

Combine all ingredients until well blended.

Place into an 8" x 8" baking pan or into a round bread loaf from which the center has been removed. Cover or wrap with foil and bake for 1 hour at 400°.

Serve with nacho chips.

Crab Dip

1 - 8 oz. pkg. cream cheese, softened
1/3 cup mayonnaise
1 Tbsp. water
1/4 tsp. onion powder
1/2 tsp. mustard
1/4 tsp. garlic, crushed
1/4 tsp. salt
1/4 tsp. Old Bay Seasoning, (or more to taste)
1/2 tsp. fresh parsley

1 - 6 to 7 1/2 oz. canned crab meat
1 cup shredded cheddar cheese

In a large mixing bowl, blend the cream cheese and mayonnaise with the seasonings.

Add the crab meat and cheese to the above mixture and stir gently to mix. Place in a 1 qt. baking dish and bake at 300° for 40 - 45 min. Serve with fancy crackers while still warm.

-Ruth

Crabmeat In a Blanket

Great for Parties

4 oz. cream cheese, softened
1/3 cup whipping cream
1 clove garlic, minced

Place first 3 ingredients into mixing bowl and blend together on medium speed until smooth.

1/2 pound fresh or canned crab meat
1/3 cup chopped pecans
3 Tbsp. chopped chives
1/4 tsp. salt
1/4 tsp. pepper

Add all the next 5 ingredients to the cream cheese mixture and blend on low speed.

28 slices sandwich bread

Trim crust from bread. Use rolling pin to flatten each slice to 1/8" thickness, then cut into 4 equal squares.

1/2 cup melted butter
Fresh parsley sprigs

Place a tsp. of the crab and cream cheese mixture on each square, fold opposite corners of bread to overlap in center. Secure with wooden toothpicks. Place on ungreased baking sheet, brush tops with the melted butter.

Bake at 325° for 20 - 25 min. until lightly browned. Remove picks and insert a stem of parsley in its place. Serve immediately.

Makes 28 appetizers.

-Marti

Party Cheese Ball

2 (8 oz.) pkgs. cream cheese, softened
2 cups shredded cheddar cheese

Combine the cheeses and mix well.

1 Tbsp. chopped pimiento
1 Tbsp. chopped green pepper
1 Tbsp. chopped onion
2 tsp. Worcestershire sauce
1 tsp. lemon juice
dash of red pepper
dash of salt

Add all these ingredients to the cheese mixture and mix together until well blended.

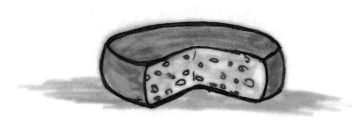

Chill in the refrigerator for a couple of hours or overnight in a covered bowl.

1/2 - 1 cup finely chopped pecans

Remove from refrigerator and shape into a ball. Roll through the nuts until it is completely coated.

Serve with fancy crackers.

-Ruth

Sausage Balls

2 lb. hot sausage, browned
2 lb. shredded sharp cheddar
    cheese
4 cups Bisquick mix
1/2 tsp. red pepper

*Combine all ingredients and mix
well. Shape into 1" balls. Place on
baking sheet and bake at 325° for
8 - 10 min.*

For a milder sausage ball, use
mild sausage and medium
cheddar cheese.

Makes about 6 doz. 1" balls.

Holiday Ham Balls

3 cups Bisquick mix
1 1/2 cups finely chopped
    smoked ham
4 cups shredded cheddar cheese
1/2 cup grated parmesan cheese
1 Tbsp. parsley flakes
2 tsp. prepared mustard
2/3 cup milk

*Mix all the ingredients together, and
roll into 1" - 1 1/2" balls. Place on
a baking sheet and bake at 325° for
8-10 min. Serve warm with honey
mustard sauce.*

Makes about 6 - 7 dozen ham

I've used these recipes on holiday, wedding or shower
buffet tables. Serve them warm with a honey-mustard or
barbecue sauce, and be sure to make plenty!

-Mom

Barbecued Appetizer Meatballs

1 bag fully cooked Italian meatballs

Your favorite barbecue sauce

Place meatballs into a large baking dish and cover with the barbecue sauce.
Bake at 325° for approximately 30 - 45 minutes or until heated through.
Serve in chafing dish.

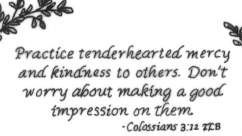

Practice tenderhearted mercy and kindness to others. Don't worry about making a good impression on them.
-Colossians 3:12 TLB

Cocktail Smokies

2 lb. pkg. Hillshire Farms 'lil smokies

1 cup barbecue sauce
1 cup concord grape jelly

Place smokies into medium saucepan.

Blend the sauce and jelly and pour over the smokies.
Simmer on stovetop till heated through.
Serve in chafing dish.

Spicy Chicken Strips

8 boneless, skinless chicken breast halves

Cut the chicken into long, thin strips (about 3/4" wide). Set aside.

3/4 cup all-purpose flour
1 tsp. chili powder
3/4 tsp. salt
1/2 tsp. garlic powder
1/4 tsp. ground cumin
1/4 tsp. pepper

Combine all these ingredients and mix well. Set aside.

1 egg, beaten
1/2 cup water

Combine the egg and water.

Vegetable oil

Dip the chicken strips into the egg mixture; then roll in flour mixture till well coated.

Fry a few strips at a time, in hot oil (375°) for 2 - 3 minutes or until golden brown. Drain on paper towels and serve immediately with the sour cream dip.

Dip:
1 cup sour cream
3 Tbsp. Dijon mustard
1 Tbsp. milk

Makes 16 appetizer servings.

*To cut the frying time you can partially cook the chicken strips before coating with the flour mixture.

Mustard

-Ruth

Vegetable Dip

1 cup sour cream
1 cup mayonnaise
3 Tbsp. parsley flakes
3 Tbsp. onion flakes
1 1/2 tsp. dill weed
1 1/2 tsp. Beau Monde
    seasoning*

Blend all ingredients together until smooth and creamy.
Refrigerate for several hours before serving for best flavor.

Makes 1 pint.

* Even though this seasoning is not a popular one, it can be found in most grocery stores.

Serve with:

Broccoli
Cauliflower
Green Peppers
Mushrooms
Cucumbers

Radishes
Fresh String Beans
Celery
Carrots

My mother-in-law, Edna, prepares this dip and has it on hand most of the time. All of the family says "no one can make dip like mom!"

-Carolyn

Ham and Cheese Pinwheels

2 (8 oz.) pkgs. cream cheese, softened
1 pkg. ranch dressing mix

In a mixing bowl, beat the cream cheese and dressing mix until smooth.

1/2 cup minced sweet red pepper
1/2 cup minced celery
1/4 cup minced onions
1/4 chopped stuffed olives, opt.

Add the next 4 ingredients and mix well.

1/2 lb. thinly sliced ham
1/2 lb. thinly sliced Swiss cheese
4 - 10" flour tortillas

Place one slice each of the ham and cheese on each tortilla, or enough to cover. Top with about 2/3 cup of the cream cheese mixture and spread evenly over the ham and cheese. Roll up tightly and wrap in plastic wrap. Refrigerate for at least 2 hours. Just prior to serving, slice into 1/2" thick pieces.

Serves 15 - 20

-Mom

Caramel Corn

1/2 cup light corn syrup
2 cups brown sugar
3/4 cup butter
pinch of cream of tarter

Place first four ingredients in a medium-sized sauce pan. Bring to a boil over medium heat; boil and stir constantly for 5 minutes. Remove from heat.

3/4 tsp. baking soda

Add the baking soda and stir.

6 - 7 quarts popped and lightly salted corn

Pour over the popped corn and mix well. Spread out into shallow baking pans. Bake at 250° for 45 minutes, stirring every 10 - 15 minutes.

-Ruth

Ranch Snacks

1 pkg. Hidden Valley ranch dressing mix
1/2 cup oil
1 tsp. garlic powder
1/4 tsp. dill weed
1/2 tsp. lemon pepper

Mix all these ingredients together, stirring until the dressing mix dissolves.

12 oz. pretzel twists *or*
12 oz. oyster crackers

Place the pretzels or crackers into a large mixing bowl and pour the ranch mix over them. Stir until well coated. Place into shallow baking pans and bake at 250° for 15 minutes, stirring once. Let cool and serve immediately or store in an airtight container.

-Carolyn

Party Mix

1/4 cup butter
1/4 tsp. garlic powder
1/4 tsp. onion salt
3 tsp. lemon juice
2 Tbsp. Worcestershire sauce

Melt butter in small saucepan, then add the remaining ingredients. Stirring until well mixed. Remove from heat.

7 cups Crispix cereal
1 1/2 cups mixed nuts,
    peanuts, or cashews
2 cups pretzel sticks
2 cups Cheerios cereal

Place all the dry ingredients in a large mixing bowl and pour the butter mixture over them. Stir until all pieces are well coated, being careful not to crush the cereal. Place on 2 large baking sheets and bake at 250° for 45 minutes, stirring every 15 minutes. Place on paper towels to cool, then serve or place in an airtight container.

This is a delicious mixture to make at Christmas time to give as gifts... Put 1 - 2 cups in a clear cellophane bag and tie with raffia or any holiday ribbon. Friends will enjoy munching on something that isn't sweet!

-Carolyn

Trail Mix

Recipe #1
1 lb. M & M's
11.5 oz. peanuts
9 oz. raisins

Recipe #2
1 lb. sunflower seeds
9 oz. raisins
6 oz. bag miniature chocolate
    chips

Combine all ingredients and store in an airtight container.

These are two different variations, the first one is my husband, Jason's favorite and is a great traveling snack that doesn't melt in your hands. The second one is my brother-in-law, Jonas' favorite mix.

There are many other options for the ingredients, such as, cashews, mixed nuts, coconut, dried fruit, granola, etc.

-Carolyn

Space Food

1 cup peanut butter
1/2 cup honey
1 cup powdered milk
1 1/2 cups graham cracker
    crumbs

Mix all ingredients together in a large mixing bowl. Shape into 1" balls and wrap each one in tin foil individually. Enjoy!

This fun and easy recipe comes from my Grandma, Naomi Stoltzfus, who taught me how to make it.

-Bethany

Wedding Tea Cakes

These tea cakes have all kinds of names - Swedish Tea Cakes, sandies, lady fingers... but no matter the name, they all have the same buttery and nutty good taste.

2 1/4 cups flour
1/2 cup powdered sugar
1 cup butter, softened
1 tsp. vanilla
1/4 tsp. salt
1/2 cup chopped nuts

Powdered sugar for rolling

Mix all ingredients together by hand and roll into 1" balls. Do not press too firmly when rolling them.

Bake at 350° for 10 minutes.

While still slightly warm, roll in a small bowl of powdered sugar.

Cool completely and roll again.

Makes 3 - 4 dozen.

-Mom

Pecan Tassies

3 oz. cream cheese, softened
1/2 cup butter, softened

1 cup flour

1/8 cup pecans, chopped

Filling:
2 eggs
3/4 cup brown sugar
1 Tbsp. butter, melted
1 tsp. vanilla
dash of salt

1/8 cup pecans, chopped

Blend cheese and butter together.

Stir in flour. Chill for 1 hour. Shape into 2 dozen 1" balls and press into ungreased tart pans, forming a crust on bottoms and sides.
Divide pecans evenly on bottom of each crust.
Blend all filling ingredients together and divide evenly into the 24 crusts.

Top with the pecans and bake at 325° until lightly browned or golden.

-Ruth

Finger Jello

2 (3 oz.) boxes gelatin, any flavor
2 envelopes unflavored gelatin
    (or 1 1/2 Tbsp.bulk gelatin)
3 cups boiling water

Empty the gelatin powders into a medium-sized mixing bowl. Let your mom boil the water and add that to the gelatin mixture. Stir until the powder is all dissolved, about 2 minutes.

Grease a 9 "x 9 "x 2" pan and let your mom pour the gelatin mixture into the pan. Put it in the refrigerator to chill. When it is set up, cut into squares with a knife or use a cookie cutter to make fun shapes. Serve immediately or store in refrigerator.

He who refreshes
others will himself
be refreshed.
    -Proverbs 11:25b NIV

-Judith

21

A welcome to our house...

When you invite company into your home, there are many ways to show them they are welcomed and loved. You may want to do so by making an elaborate meal, which tells them you put a lot of thought and effort into their enjoyment. But even if you are only serving a glass of lemonade or a bowl of party mix, take the time to place a lemon slice on the rim of the glass or serve the party mix in lovely glass bowls. These little touches go a long way in the hearts of your guests, and it's such an easy way to share the gift of hospitality.

Even if you aren't serving any food or drink, having a scented candle lit, being at the door to greet them (or better yet, on the front porch!) tells them you are looking forward to their arrival.

Most importantly, relax! Don't take on a menu that is overwhelming and keeps you and your guests from enjoying the meal or social time together. After all the reason for hospitality is not to amaze people with your culinary skills, but to enjoy and build new friendships, and cultivate old ones.

You are as welcome as the flowers in May.
- William Shakespeare

Breads,
Muffins,
and
Brunches

BREADS, MUFFINS AND BRUNCHES

Basic White Bread

This recipe comes from my son-in-law, Jonas' family, the Stoltzfus'. I have been using it for nearly 15 years, and have made hundreds of loaves in our bake shop. Rarely does this standby recipe fail to turn out for me, and I use it as a base for all of our specialty breads, such as Cinnamon Raisin or Swirl, Cheddar Cheese, Garlic Onion, and Italian Cheese. Be creative and design your own favorites!

2 Tbsp. yeast
2 cups warm water
1/4 cup sugar

Combine these 3 ingredients and set aside.

2 cups milk

Scald milk in saucepan over medium heat, stirring frequently.

1 1/2 Tbsp. salt
1 egg, beaten
4 Tbsp. shortening
1/2 cup sugar

Place these ingredients in a large mixing bowl and pour the scalded milk over them. Add the yeast mixture and stir.

6 lbs. bread flour

Add the flour to the above mixture, about one cup at a time, enough to make a pliable dough that pulls away from the sides of the mixing bowl. Knead for 10 minutes, then set in a warm place and let rise for 20 min. Punch down and let rise another 15 minutes. Punch down again and shape into 1 lb. loaves, place these into bread pans and let rise again till double in size. Bake at 350° for 20 - 25 minutes, until golden brown.
Makes 5 1 lb. loaves.

-Mom

Easy Wheat Bread

4 1/2 cups warm water
3 Tbsp. instant yeast
1/2 cup canola oil
1/2 cup honey
1 Tbsp. salt
2 Tbsp. wheat gluten*
2 Tbsp. dough enhancer*
2 cups all purpose flour

6 cups (approx.) freshly ground
    Golden 86 wheat flour**

*These ingredients may be found at a bulk food store or at a specialty health food or grocery store.
**Golden 86 wheat berries can be found at some health food or bulk food stores. If your local store will grind the wheat for you, store the flour in the freezer to maintain the freshness. If you have your own grinder, buy the berries and grind only the amount of flour you need each time.
This recipe also can be made using only wheat flour and eliminating the 2 cups of white flour.

Measure the water and yeast into the mixing bowl of a heavy duty mixer. (Can also be done by hand, be sure to knead thoroughly.) Then add all the following ingredients while mixing on the 'stir' speed with the dough hook.

Increase the mixing speed to '2' and add the wheat flour one-half cupful at a time just until the dough starts to pull away from the sides of the mixing bowl. (I usually knead the last cup of flour in by hand.) Scrape into another large, greased mixing bowl, cover with a damp cloth and set in a warm place to rise. Let rise until double in size, then punch down. With oiled hands separate and shape into 4 - 5 loaves and place into greased bread pans. Prick tops of loaves with fork, cover with damp cloth and set in a warm place. Let loaves rise until they are double in size.
Bake at 325° for 20 minutes or until the tops are golden brown. Remove from oven and butter tops of the loaves. Let set in pans for 1 - 2 minutes then remove to a large bread cloth and cover loaves until partially cooled. (Placing the loaves into bread bags while still slightly warm makes a softer loaf.)
Freeze loaves that will not be used within 12 - 24 hours.

Carolyn

Honey Wheat Bread

For a Bread Machine

1/2 cup buttermilk
1/4 cup water
1 Tbsp. butter flavored
    shortening

Combine the first 3 ingredients in a microwave safe bowl and heat in microwave until shortening is melted. Pour into the bottom of bread machine.

3 Tbsp. honey
1/2 tsp. sugar
1 tsp. salt
1 egg

Add the next 4 ingredients and stir slightly.

1 pkg. (3 tsp.) yeast

Add the yeast and stir until yeast is dissolved.

2 1/4 cups bread flour
1/2 cup whole wheat flour

Pour the flour over the liquid ingredients.

Set bread machine for 1.5 lb. loaf, light crust and start.

When you remove the bread, spray lightly with a baking spray.

Yields 1 loaf.

-Marti

Dinner Rolls

1 Tbsp. yeast
1 Tbsp. sugar
1/2 cup warm water (105°-115°)

Mix the yeast and sugar with the water and let it set for 5 - 10 minutes.

1 cup warm water
1/3 cup sugar
1/2 cup vegetable oil
1 1/4 tsp. salt
4 1/2 cups flour

Meanwhile mix the water, sugar, oil and salt.
Add the dissolved yeast mixture, mix well and add 2 1/2 cups of the flour; mix well.

If you are mixing the dough in an electric mixer, switch to the dough hook , add the remaining 2 cups of flour and knead for 4 - 5 minutes. If you are mixing the dough by hand, add the remaining flour and mix well and continue to knead for 5 - 7 minutes.

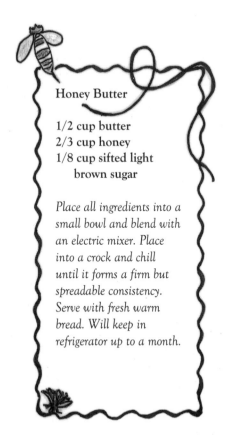

Honey Butter

1/2 cup butter
2/3 cup honey
1/8 cup sifted light
     brown sugar

Place all ingredients into a small bowl and blend with an electric mixer. Place into a crock and chill until it forms a firm but spreadable consistency. Serve with fresh warm bread. Will keep in refrigerator up to a month.

Cover the dough and let rise for 1 hour or until doubled in size. Punch down and let rise for another 1/2 hour.
Butter two 9" pie or cake pans generously. Divide the dough into half and shape into 12 dinner rolls per pan.
Or butter two bread pans and shape into 2 - 1 pound loaves. Cover and let rise until double in size.

Bake at 325° for 25 - 30 minutes or until nicely browned.

Ruth

Variations for the Dinner Rolls

Cinnamon Swirl Bread

One recipe Dinner Roll dough
for two loaves, pg. 28

Cinnamon
Sugar
Softened butter

Follow directions on page 28, down
to dividing into 2 equal parts. Roll
each part out into oblong shape,
about 6"x9" and brush with the
softened butter. Sprinkle with the
cinnamon and sugar mixture to
taste. Roll up the dough tightly,
starting at the 6" end.
Place into greased bread pans, and
let rise until double. Bake at 325°
for 20 - 25 minutes, or until tops
are golden brown. Brush with butter
and remove from pans onto a
cooling rack.

Monkey Bread

One recipe Dinner Roll dough,
pg. 28
1/2 cup butter

Follow the dinner roll recipe to
shaping into the rolls, then take
each roll and dip it into the melted
butter. Stack them into several
small, greased crocks, let rise until
double in size. Bake at 325° for 25
minutes or until golden brown.

Wheat Dinner Rolls

Simply replace the flour in recipe on pg. 28 to all or part wheat flour. To
make pumpernickel or rye rolls, replace 1/2 - 1 cup of the white flour with the
flour of your choice.

~Ruth

Parmesan Cheddar Braid

1 cup milk
1/2 cup butter
1/3 cup sugar

2/3 cup sugar
2 tsp. salt
1/2 tsp. soda
1/2 cup hot mashed potatoes

1 1/2 cups cold water
4 egg yolks, beaten

2 Tbsp. instant yeast
2 cups bread flour

5 1/2 - 6 cups bread flour

4 Tbsp. butter, melted
1 1/3 finely shredded cheddar
   cheese
1/2 cup parmesan

This bread is the perfect complement for spaghetti, lasagna or pizza. Freeze extra loaves or share with a friend.
Dough can also be used for dinner or cinnamon rolls. Mix once and create a variety of breads from the same dough!

Scald milk with butter and sugar. Set aside.

Combine the next four ingredients into the mixing bowl of a heavy duty mixer. Pour scalded milk over this mixture; beat until well blended.

Add water and mix then add the beaten egg yolks.

Combine the yeast and flour; gradually add to the liquid mixture while beating on low speed with dough hooks. Continue adding flour slowly until dough begins to pull away from the sides of mixing bowl. Dough will be somewhat sticky. Continue kneading for 3 - 5 minutes.
Place dough into a greased bowl; cover and let rise for 45 minutes - 1 hour. Divide dough in half. Roll out each half to a rectangle approximately 12"x24". Brush each rectangle with 2 Tbsp. of the butter and sprinkle with the cheeses, dividing evenly between the two.
Begin to roll from the wide side; ending seam side down. With a sharp knife; cut into roll (as for cinnamon rolls, but not cutting all the way through) every 1 1/2 - 2 inches apart. After 5 cuts; make a complete cut to make a loaf. Transfer to a greased baking sheet. Sprinkle with more parmesan cheese. Let rise until double in size, about 20 - 30 minutes. Bake at 350° for 25 minutes or until lightly browned. Brush tops of warm bread for a soft crust. Cover until cooled.

-Kathleen

Zucchini Bread

3 eggs
2 cups white sugar

Beat the eggs, then add the sugar; cream until light.

1 cup all-purpose flour
1 cup wheat flour
1/2 tsp. soda
1 tsp. cinnamon
1 tsp. salt
1 tsp. vanilla
1 cup canola oil

Sift the dry ingredients together and add to the creamed mixture alternating with the oil and vanilla. Mix well.

1 cup Quaker quick oats
2 cups zucchini, shredded

1/2 cup miniature chocolate
  chips, divided, opt.
1/2 cup chopped pecans, opt.

Fold in the oats and zucchini, mixing just until well blended. Pour into 2 greased loaf pans. Sprinkle 1/4 cup of the chocolate chips and nuts over the top of each loaf.
Bake at 350° for 50 - 55 minutes, or until tester comes out clean.

Makes 2 loaves.

This recipe can be enjoyed year round by shredding your excess zucchini in the summer time. Simply place two cups in a Ziploc freezer bag and freeze until ready to use. Let thaw before adding, it will appear very watery, but do not drain the liquid.

~Carolyn

Banana Nut Bread

1 2/3 cup sugar
3 - 4 ripe, mashed bananas

Cream the sugar and bananas together.

2 eggs
1/2 cup butter
1/2 cup oil

Add these ingredients to the creamed mixture and mix well.

2 cups flour
3 tsp. baking powder
1 tsp. salt

Sift the dry ingredients together and add to the creamed mixture.

1 tsp. vanilla
1 cup chopped nuts

Add the vanilla and nuts to the above mixture and mix well. Pour into 2 loaf pans.
Bake at 325° for 50 minutes or until tester comes out clean. Remove to cooling racks.

Makes 2 loaves.

My sister-in-law, Sonya, shared this moist and delicious bread recipe with me. The recipe comes from her mom who got it from a neighbor, etc. Once when she and my brother-in-law, Marcus were up to visit, (they live in Georgia) she prepared this for us. It was a delightful treat, not only because it was delicious, but also because it's only special house guests who make themselves at home in your kitchen and prepare something for you!

~Carolyn

Angel Biscuits

2 cups flour
4 tsp. baking powder
1/2 tsp. salt
1 Tbsp. sugar, optional

Sift the first 4 ingredients together.

4 Tbsp. butter flavored
   shortening

*Add the shortening and mix well
with your hands.*

3/4 cup milk

*Pour milk over the above mixture
and knead lightly just until the
dough is evenly moist. Turn onto a
floured surface and sprinkle the top
of the dough lightly with flour. Roll
out to about 1/2" thickness. Cut
out shapes with a round cookie
cutter.*
*Place the biscuits 1" apart on an
ungreased baking sheet. Bake at
400° for 10 minutes or until lightly
browned.*

These biscuits are great to
use at a theme party! For
example, on Valentines
Day use a heart cutter.
You can vary this for
whatever is appropriate for
your special occasion.

~Hannah

Bisquick Variations

For all the following variations, start out with the basic Bisquick biscuit recipe. Just add these extra ingredients and follow the mixing and baking directions on the box.

1 cup shredded cheddar cheese
1/2 tsp. garlic

3 Tbsp. melted butter

After removing biscuits from the oven, brush with the melted butter and serve immediately.
Serve with chili or lasagna.

1 tsp. finely chopped onion
1 tsp. dill weed

This is delicious served with chicken noodle soup!

1/4 cup extra Bisquick mix
1/2 cup salsa

Serve this variation with any Mexican dish.

~Marti

Caramel Apple Cheese Danish

1 (10 count) roll Pillsbury
    refrigerator biscuits

Press the biscuits into a greased 9"x13" cake pan.

1 (8 oz.) cream cheese, softened
1/2 cup powdered sugar
1 tsp. vanilla

Mix these three ingredients until creamy. Spread over the biscuits.

1 Granny Smith apple, chopped
1/2 cup chopped pecans

Sprinkle the apple pieces and pecans over the cream cheese mixture.

cinnamon
1/2 - 3/4 cup caramel ice cream
    topping

Sprinkle with cinnamon to taste and drizzle the caramel topping over everything.
Bake at 350° for 15 - 20 minutes.

Serve warm with ice cream or Cool Whip.

**Love is sweet, but
it's nice to have
bread with it.**
-Yiddish Wisdom

~Marti

Cinnamon Rolls

1 cup warm water (105°- 115°)
2 Tbsp. yeast

Dissolve the yeast in the water and set aside.

1 cup milk
1/2 cup butter

Heat milk with the butter in a small saucepan until the butter is melted and mixture is slightly scalded.

1/2 cup sugar
1 1/2 tsp. salt

Place the sugar and salt in a large mixing bowl and stir in the milk mixture.

2 eggs, slightly beaten

Add the eggs. Let cool to lukewarm. Add the yeast mixture and stir.

5 - 6 cups flour

Add flour one cup at a time, kneading well after each addition. Use only enough flour so that the dough can be handled, leaving it as sticky as possible. Cover and let rise 1 1/2 - 2 hours or until doubled in size.

1/2 cup butter, divided and softened
brown sugar
cinnamon

Punch down and divide the dough evenly into two parts and on a lightly floured surface shape each part into approximately an 8"x15" rectangular shape with a rolling pin or your hands.

Makes 4 - 8" round pans.

Brush with the softened butter and sprinkle with the brown sugar and cinnamon to taste. Roll up the dough starting at the 15" end of the rectangular piece. With a sharp knife; slice through roll every 1" - 1 1/2" and place 5 - 6 slices into greased 8" round pans with edges only slightly touching. Let rise about one hour or until doubled in size.
Bake at 325° for 20 minutes, or just until golden brown.
Cool and ice (see page 37 for icing recipes).

-Carolyn

Icing for Cinnamon Rolls

Powdered Sugar Glaze Icing

2 cups powdered sugar
3 - 4 Tbsp. milk
1 1/2 tsp. vanilla

Mix all these ingredients together until smooth and spread over the cinnamon rolls.

Caramel Icing

1/2 cup butter
1/4 cup milk
1 cup brown sugar
1 tsp. vanilla

Melt butter in saucepan and add the brown sugar, stir and cook for 1 minute. Add the vanilla.

3 cups powdered sugar

Let cool, then add the powdered sugar while mixing. It may take slightly more or less powdered sugar to bring it to a spreading consistency. Spread on slightly warm cinnamon rolls.

Maple Icing

1 1/2 lbs. powdered sugar
1/4 cup butter
1/3 cup water
1/4 tsp. vanilla butternut
    flavoring (McNess
    product)
1/4 cup Crisco
3/4 tsp. maple flavoring
1 tsp. cornstarch

Combine all ingredients in a large mixing bowl and blend until smooth.

Spread over warm cinnamon rolls and top with chopped nuts.

Sugar and Spice Muffins

1 3/4 cups flour
1 1/2 tsp. baking powder
1/2 tsp. salt
1/2 tsp. nutmeg

Combine the dry ingredients.

1/2 cup vegetable oil
3/4 cup sugar
1 egg
3/4 cup milk

In a separate bowl, combine the oil, sugar, egg and milk, mixing well. Add this to the dry ingredients stirring gently just until all ingredients are combined. Line a muffin tin with paper baking cups and fill 2/3 of cup with the muffin batter. Bake at 350° for 18 minutes.

Topping;
1/4 cup butter, melted

3/4 cup sugar, combined with;
1 tsp. cinnamon

Remove from oven and immediately dip the top of each muffin into the melted butter, then roll in the sugar and cinnamon mixture. Serve immediately or store in an airtight container.

Makes 1 dozen muffins.

My sister-in-law, Anne Miller, can always be counted on to prepare tempting-to-the-sweet-tooth desserts. She is also an expert muffin maker, this recipe is one of hers. She says the secret to her light muffins is in not over-mixing the batter. However she does it, they are delicious!

~Carolyn

Cinnamon Bran Muffins

This recipe makes a large amount of muffin batter, but the batter keeps very well in the refrigerator for up to a week, to be used for several meals. These muffins are delicious served warm with apple butter, or along with soups, and any spicy foods. A good recipe to make a day or two ahead to avoid that last minute rush!

1 cup warm water
1 cup bran flakes
1/2 cup butter, melted

Pour the warm water and melted butter over the bran flakes and set aside.

2 eggs
1 1/2 cups sugar

Beat the eggs well, then add the sugar and cream.

2 1/2 cups all-purpose flour
2 1/2 tsp. baking soda
1/2 tsp. salt
1 1/2 tsp. cinnamon
2 cups milk

Sift the dry ingredients together, and add to the creamed mixture, alternating with the milk.

2 cups quick oatmeal

Add the oatmeal, mixing just until well blended, then fold in the bran mixture. Do not overmix.
Fill greased muffin tins about 1/2 full with batter and bake at 400° for 15 - 20 minutes.

Makes approximately 24 - 28 muffins.

~Carolyn

Saturday Pancakes

In my growing up years, I often spent the night with my friend Wanda (Overholt) Steiner. I always enjoyed any time I spent with her family, but it was a special bonus when my stay-over was on a Friday night and I could be there for their family tradition of Saturday morning pancakes. Jason and I have picked up this tradition and in our search for that 'perfect pancake' we both have tried numerous recipes and mixes. This has been our favorite.

1 cup all-purpose flour
2 Tbsp. sugar
1 1/2 Tbsp. baking powder
1/2 tsp. salt

Combine all dry ingredients.

1 egg
2 Tbsp. butter flavored
   shortening, melted
3/4 cup milk, approximately

Beat egg slightly with a fork, then add to the dry mixture along with the shortening and milk. Add just enough milk to make the batter pour easily, it may take a little more or less. Mix together with fork until well blended but not overmixed. Will be slightly lumpy and foamy. Bake on a griddle heated to 300° degrees.

Makes about 8 - 4" pancakes.

Happy is the house that shelters a friend.
-Ralph Waldo Emerson

~Carolyn

Baked Oatmeal

1 cup brown sugar
1/2 cup butter, softened
2 eggs, beaten

Cream sugar and butter together until light. Then add the eggs and mix well.

3 cups quick oats
2 tsp. baking powder
1 cup milk
1/4 tsp. salt

Add the baking powder and salt, then alternately add the oats and milk, mixing just until well blended. Pour into a greased 9"x9" baking dish and bake at 350° for 30 minutes. Serve this warm with milk for a breakfast dish, or with ice cream for a dessert.

Credit for this recipe goes to Sharon Troyer, a friend from Indiana. She enjoys cooking and always has tasty meals and snacks to serve when we visit them.

~Carolyn

Breakfast Pizza

1 (8 oz.) pkg. refrigerated
   crescent rolls

Separate the crescent rolls into 8 triangles, with the elongated points pointing to the center of a lightly greased 12" pizza pan. Press and seal to form a crust and rim. Bake at 375° for 5 - 6 minutes. Remove. Reduce heat to 350°.

1 Tbsp. butter
1 medium green pepper,
   chopped
1 (6 oz.) pkg. Canadian bacon,
   chopped *or* 8 - 10 slices
   regular bacon, fried and
   crumbled
1/2 tsp. oregano

Sauté the green pepper, bacon and oregano in the butter in a large skillet for 2 minutes. Arrange half of this mixture on top of the crust.

6 small potatoes, cooked and
   sliced to 1/4"
1 cup Colby Jack cheese,
   shredded
1 cup cheddar cheese,
   shredded

Top with the potato slices and sprinkle 1/2 cup each of the two cheeses on top of the potatoes.

5 eggs, beaten,
1/2 cup milk
1/4 tsp. pepper
1/2 tsp. salt

Combine these ingredients, stir well. Pour over the pizza. Sprinkle with the remaining sautéed mixture and cheeses. Bake at 350° for 30 - 35 minutes.

Serves 6 - 8.

~Ruth

Company Egg Omelet

6 slices white bread, crusts
   removed and cubed
1 lb. ham slices, chopped
1/4 cup mushrooms
1/4 cup green peppers
bits of tomato for color, (opt.)

Place the bread pieces in a greased 9"x13" baking dish and sprinkle the ham, mushrooms and green peppers over the bread. Add chopped tomatoes for color, if desired.

6 eggs
2 cups milk
1 tsp. salt
1 tsp. dry mustard
1/4 tsp. black pepper

Beat eggs slightly and add the remaining ingredients, beating until well blended. Pour over the bread in baking pan.

1 cup cheddar cheese, shredded
fresh parsley for garnish

Top with the cheese and bake at 350° for 45 minutes. This recipe can also be mixed the evening before and refrigerated. Remove from refrigerator about 15 - 20 minutes before baking. Garnish with parsley after baking as desired.

Serves 10.

The Crown of the house
is Godliness.
The Beauty of the house
is Order.
The Glory of the house
is Hospitality.
The Blessing of the house
is Contentment.
Old Inscription

~Mom

Arlington Brunch

12 slices white bread
6 slices luncheon ham
6 slices American cheese
butter

Remove crusts from the bread and arrange 6 slices in a greased 9"x13" baking dish. Layer the ham and cheese on top on the bread. Spread one side of the remaining 6 pieces of bread with butter and place them on the ham with buttered side down.

6 eggs
3 cups milk
1 tsp. dry mustard

Beat the eggs and add the mustard and milk. Pour over the bread, cover and chill overnight.

1/2 cup butter, melted
1 cup crushed corn flakes

Mix the corn flakes and butter until the crumbs are well coated. Sprinkle this mixture on top and bake at 350° for one hour or until set.

This is a convenient breakfast recipe since it can be made the day or evening before. The recipe comes from my sister-in-law, Rachel, who got it from her Aunt Ruth.

Carolyn

Quiche

1 unbaked pie shell

If frozen, remove from freezer.

5 eggs, beaten
1 cup milk
1 tsp. salt
1/2 tsp. pepper
1 Tbsp. Worcestershire sauce
1 cup bacon, fried and cut into
    small pieces
1/2 cup chopped tomatoes
1/4 cup chopped onion
1/2 cup grated cheddar cheese

*Beat the eggs well, and add the rest
of the ingredients. Mix well and
pour into the unbaked pie shell.
Bake at 350° for 40 - 45 minutes*

Serves 6

Variation:
Omit the bacon and add:
    1 cup broccoli, chopped
    1 cup grated cheddar
      cheese

This is a dish that we made for a local Bed & Breakfast.
They served it with a slice of tomato and some fresh fruit
for a luncheon plate.

-Mom

Breakfast Casserole

5 eggs
1 1/4 cup water
1 cup milk

Beat the eggs; then add the water and milk and mix well.

3 cups boiled, shredded
    potatoes*
1 1/2 cup shredded cheddar
    cheese
1 1/2 cup ground sausage,
    browned
1/4 cup chopped onion
1/4 tsp. black pepper
1 tsp. salt
1 tsp. parsley flakes

Add the remaining ingredients and stir until thoroughly mixed. Pour into an ungreased 9"x13" baking dish. Bake uncovered at 350° for 40 - 45 minutes, or until set.

Serves 8.

* For a quick potato substitution I use the frozen, southern style hashbrowns, and add only 3/4 cup of water instead of 1 1/4.

Variation:
    Add 3/4 cup of cooked, crumbled bacon instead of the sausage; or 1 cup fully cooked ham cubes.

-Carolyn

Pecan Coffee Ring

This is a quick and easy recipe!

1 Tbsp. butter, melted	*Brush a 10" tube pan with the butter.*
2 Tbsp. butter, melted **3 Tbsp. maple syrup**	*In a small bowl, combine the syrup and butter.* *Drizzle 2 Tbsp. into pan.*
1/4 cup brown sugar **1/4 cup pecans, chopped** **1/2 tsp. cinnamon**	*Combine the sugar, pecans and cinnamon. Sprinkle half of mixture over the syrup mixture in pan.*
1 (12 oz.) tube refrigerated **buttermilk biscuits**	*Separate biscuits, place into prepared pan with edges overlapping.* *Top with remaining syrup and nut mixture.*
	Bake at 375° for 20 - 25 minutes, or until golden brown. *Cool for 1 - 2 minutes. Invert onto a serving platter.* *Serve warm.*

Serves 10.

-Ruth

Tips for Making House Guests Feel At Home

Leave a selection of magazines and some favorite books on your guest bedside table.

Place a fresh bouquet of flowers in the guest room.

Turn down the guest bed and place a mint or chocolate on the pillow.

Make sure there is an alarm clock and a box of tissues in the room.

Place fresh towels and soap where guests can easily find them. Also keep a few extra toiletries available in case your guest has forgotten an item.

Have coffee brewing in the morning before your guests make an appearance, if available place a newspaper nearby.

Be available and flexible to accommodate your guests.

If you are cooking for your guests, be sure to be aware of any special food needs, such as allergies, diabetes, etc.

Soups,
Sandwiches,
and
Salads

SOUPS, SALADS AND SANDWICHES

Marti's Gumbo

2 cans (14 oz.) chicken broth
1 can (14 1/2 oz.) diced tomatoes
1 can (14 1/2 oz.) tomato sauce
3 cups water
1 can (15 oz.) whole kernel corn
1 medium onion, chopped
2 cloves garlic, minced
2 stalks celery, chopped
1 (16 oz.) bag frozen okra or
   field peas
1/2 lb. sausage ring, cut into
   small pieces*
1/2 cup butter
salt and pepper to taste
1 tsp. hot sauce or 1 tsp. cayenne
   pepper

Mix all these ingredients in a large pot, bring to a boil and let boil for 5 minutes.

1 cup uncooked rice

Add the rice, cover and simmer for 20 minutes.

1/2 lb. shrimp, peeled and
   de-veined*

Add the shrimp to the pot and continue simmering until the shrimp are pink.

*If you prefer using only shrimp or sausage instead of both; simply add 1 lb. of the preferred meat.

If you want more liquid in your soup, just add water until you have the right consistency. We like ours thick, served over cornbread.

Marti

Chicken Noodle Soup

This is very easy recipe and quick to make. Biscuits are delicious served with this soup!

2 cans (14 oz.) chicken broth
2 cups water
1/2 cup chopped onion
2 garlic cloves, minced, or 2 tsp. garlic powder
1/2 tsp. basil
salt and pepper to taste
2 boneless chicken breasts, cut into small pieces
1 large potato, cubed, 1/2 inch pieces
1 can (15 oz.) whole kernel corn *or* 1 pint frozen corn
1/4 cup butter

5 to 8 oz. wide noodles, (more for a thicker soup, less for more broth)

Place all ingredients except the noodles into a large pot. Bring to a boil and boil for about 5 minutes.

Add the noodles and simmer until noodles are tender and chicken is cooked.

Marti

Potato Bacon Chowder

8 slices bacon, cut into 1" pieces
2 Tbsp. butter
2 cups cubed 1/2" new red
    potatoes
1/2 cup chopped onions
1/4 tsp. celery seed
salt and pepper to taste

In a 3-qt. saucepan cook bacon over medium heat for 5 minutes; add the butter, potatoes, onions and seasonings. Continue cooking, stirring occasionally, until the potatoes are tender, 15 - 20 minutes.

1 cup sour cream
2 cups milk
1 can (10 3/4 oz.) condensed
    cream of chicken soup
1 can (8 oz.) whole kernel corn,
    drained
1/4 tsp. thyme leaves

Add these remaining ingredients and continue cooking, stirring occasionally, until heated through 10 -12 minutes.

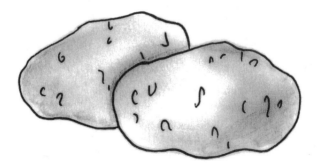

-Ruth

Cheeseburger Soup

1/2 lb. ground beef

On a stovetop skillet, brown the beef, drain and set aside.

3/4 cup chopped onion
3/4 cup shredded carrots
3/4 cup diced celery
1 tsp. dried basil
1 tsp. dried parsley flakes
1 Tbsp. butter or margarine

In the same skillet, sauté the vegetables and herbs in the butter, until the vegetables are tender, about
5 - 7 minutes.

3 cups chicken broth
3 1/2 cups peeled and cubed
    (1/2") potatoes
1/2 tsp. garlic powder
1/4 tsp. chili powder
1/2 tsp. celery salt
1/2 tsp. salt
dash of pepper

While the vegetables are cooking, place the broth in a 3-qt. saucepan, bring to a boil and add the potatoes and seasonings. Reduce heat, cover and simmer for approximately
8 - 10 minutes until potatoes are tender. Do not drain. Add the sautéed vegetables and beef.

1/4 cup all purpose flour
3 Tbsp. butter

Melt the butter in skillet. Add flour; cook and stir for 1 - 2 minutes or until bubbly. Add to soup and bring to a boil. Cook and stir for 2 minutes.

1 1/2 cups milk
3/4 cup shredded cheddar
    cheese
1 cup cubed Velveeta cheese

Add the milk and cheeses; cook and stir until the cheese melts. Remove from heat.

Makes 4 main dish servings.

-Carolyn

Crab or Tuna Chowder

6 slices bacon, cut into 1" pieces
2 cups cubed potatoes
1/2 cup chopped onion
1/2 cup chopped celery

3 Tbsp. butter
3 Tbsp. flour

3 cups milk
1 - (6 oz.) can canned crab or
    tuna
1/2 tsp. basil
pinch of cayenne pepper
1 tsp. parsley flakes
salt and pepper to taste

3/4 cup cheddar cheese,
    shredded

In 3 qt. saucepan, cook bacon over medium heat for 5 minutes, add potatoes, onion and celery. Continue cooking, stirring occasionally, until vegetables are tender.

While above mixture is cooking, melt butter in small saucepan. Stir in flour until smooth and bubbly, add to the potato mixture

Add remaining ingredients, cook over medium heat until heated through.

Sprinkle cheese over soup just prior to serving.

-Ruth

Cheese-Broccoli Soup

1 3/4 cups chicken broth
1 cup peeled & diced potatoes
1/2 cup finely shredded carrots
1/2 cup finely chopped celery
1/4 cup finely chopped onion
1/4 - 1/2 cup finely chopped
   broccoli
1/2 tsp. salt
1/4 tsp. pepper
1/8 tsp. celery seed

In a medium saucepan combine the broth, potatoes, carrots, celery, onion, broccoli and seasonings. Bring to a boil, then reduce heat. Cover and simmer for 10 - 15 minutes or until vegetables are tender. Using the back of a fork, slightly mash the vegetables against the side of the saucepan.

Option: I like to put all the vegetables in my food processor & chop them coarsely before cooking.

2 cups milk
3 Tbsp. cornstarch

Combine 1/4 cup milk and cornstarch in a small bowl and mix until smooth. Stir into the soup and add remaining milk.
Cook and stir until thick and bubbly.

1 cup shredded cheddar cheese

Add cheese and stir until melted.

56

-Ruth

Cheesy Chowder

2 1/2 cups water
2 cups diced potatoes
1/2 cup diced carrots
1/2 cup diced celery
1 tsp. salt
1/4 tsp. pepper

Combine water, potatoes, carrots, celery, salt and pepper in a large kettle. Cook 10 - 12 minutes or until vegetables are tender. Do not drain.

White Sauce:
1/4 cup butter
1/4 cup flour
2 cups milk
1 cup grated cheddar cheese
1 cup Velveeta cheese, cubed

Meanwhile, in small saucepan melt the butter; add flour and stir and cook until smooth and bubbly. Stirring with wire whisk, slowly add milk; cook until thickened. Add grated cheese and stir until melted.

2 cups cubed, cooked ham

Remove from heat; add the cubed ham. Add this sauce to the cooked vegetable mixture, heat and serve.

Serves 6.

-Hannah

Turkey Cheddar Chowder

Use above recipe and add:

1/2 tsp. poultry seasoning
dash of garlic
1/4 tsp. celery seed,
to the vegetable mixture

2 cups cubed, cooked turkey
(in place of the ham) to the white sauce mixture

-Carolyn

Tomato - Pasta Soup

2 Tbsp. butter
2 cloves garlic
1/4 medium onion
1 medium carrot
2 stalks celery

Chop garlic, onion, celery, carrot finely. Melt the butter in a heavy saucepan and sauté the vegetables until tender.

1 (10 3/4 oz.) can tomato soup
1 (13 3/4 oz.) can chicken broth
2 1/2 - 3 cups tomato juice
1 tsp. oregano
1/2 tsp. celery seed
salt and pepper, to taste

Add the soup, broth, juice and seasonings, bring to a slow boil and add the pasta. Cook until pasta is tender.

1/4 cup mini bow tie pasta

Optional: for a smooth tomato soup; eliminate pasta and puree in blender.

This soup is delicious served with toasted cheese sandwiches and a side of raw vegetables or a tossed salad.

-Ruth

Slow Cooked Chili

2 lbs. ground beef

Brown the beef in a skillet, drain. Transfer to a slow cooker.

2 (16 oz.) cans kidney beans, rinsed and drained*
2 (14 1/2 oz.) cans diced tomatoes, undrained
1 (8 oz.) can tomato sauce
2 medium onions, chopped
2 medium potatoes, diced, optional
1 green pepper, chopped
2 garlic cloves, minced
2 Tbsp. chili powder
2 tsp. salt, or to taste
1 tsp. pepper

Add these next 10 ingredients to the slow cooker. Cover and cook on low heat for 8 - 10 hours, or on high for 4 hours.

Cheddar cheese shredded

Garnish with the shredded cheese just prior to serving.

*other canned beans of your choice can be substituted

-Marti

Mexican Chicken'n Cheese Soup

1/4 cup butter
1/2 cup green bell pepper, diced
1/2 cup onion, minced

Melt butter in a large saucepan, add the peppers and onions. Sauté 3 - 4 minutes until tender.

1/3 cup flour

Add the flour, stirring constantly.

2 (10 1/2 oz.) cans chicken broth

Gradually add the broth and simmer, stirring constantly until thickened. Reduce heat.

2 cups cooked and diced chicken breasts
1 (4.5 oz.) can chopped green chilis
1/2 tsp. cumin
1/2 tsp. oregano
1/2 tsp. red pepper

Stir in the chicken, chilis and seasonings and heat thoroughly.

1 cup milk
4 cups Monterey Jack cheese, grated

Add the cheese and milk, stirring while adding. Simmer for 5 minutes or until heated.

Fried Tortilla Strips:
3 - 4 corn or flour tortillas
butter

Fry the tortillas in butter till crisp. Slice into thin strips and serve alongside or sprinkle over the soup.

-Ruth

Brunswick Stew

5 - 6 skinless, boneless chicken
  breasts
1 1/2 lbs. pork loin

*Place chicken and pork in an 8-qt.
or larger stockpot; cover 1/3 way
with water. Cook until tender
(approx. 45 - 60 minutes); remove
meat from liquid and shred with
fork. Reserve stock in pot.*

3 quarts canned tomatoes
1 large onion, chopped
1 1/2 cups ketchup
1/4 cup Worcestershire sauce

*Add tomatoes, onions, ketchup,
Worcestershire sauce and shredded
meat to stock in pot and cook until
stew thickens (approximately 1 1/2
hours). Cook slowly and stir often.*

1 (15 oz.) cans butter beans
1 (15 oz.) cans whole kernel corn
salt and pepper
1 1/2 cups diced potatoes
1/4 lb. butter

*Add beans, corn, salt, pepper,
potatoes and butter. Cook until
potatoes are done.*

Serves approximately 15 - 20.

I have seen many versions of this stew, but this one has
certainly been our favorite and was shared with us from a
dear friend, Brenda Galbreath. Just as we made a few
changes from the original to suit our family's taste, you
can add or subtract according to your own taste!

-Ruth

Shredded Barbecue Beef

1 - 4 lb. boneless beef chuck roast
1 Tbsp. cooking oil

In Dutch oven, brown roast on all sides in oil.

2 Tbsp. cooking oil
2 large onions, chopped

In a large saucepan; sauté onions in oil until tender.

1 cup ketchup
1 beef broth
2/3 cup chili sauce
1/4 cup vinegar
1/4 cup brown sugar
3 Tbsp. Worcestershire sauce
2 Tbsp. prepared mustard
2 Tbsp. honey
2 Tbsp. lemon juice
1 tsp. salt
1/4 tsp. cayenne pepper
1/8 tsp. pepper
1 Tbsp. liquid smoke

Add remaining ingredients to the onions. Bring to a boil; reduce heat; simmer for 15 minutes, stirring occasionally. Pour over roast. Cover and bake at 325° for 4 hours, or until meat is very tender. Remove roast, shred with fork and return to sauce.

12 hamburger buns

Serve on rolls.

Makes approx. 12 sandwiches.

-Marti

Slow Cooked Barbecue Sandwich Recipes

Barbecue Beef 'n Pork

1 1/2 lbs. stew beef
1 1/2 lbs. pork cubes
1 cup chopped onion
1 (6 oz.) can tomato paste
1/2 cup brown sugar
1/4 cup vinegar
3 Tbsp. chili powder
2 tsp. salt
1 tsp. dry mustard
1 1/2 tsp. Worcestershire sauce
1/4 cup water

Combine all ingredients in a 5 qt. slow cooker. Cook on low for 6 - 8 hours. Shred meat with a fork and place on buns with lettuce and tomatoes.

Makes 12 sandwiches.

Barbecue Pork

2 - 3 lbs. roast pork
1 cup ketchup
1 cup water
1/2 tsp. salt
1/4 tsp. paprika
1/3 cup mustard
1 small chopped onion
1/2 tsp. pepper
1 Tbsp. hot pepper
dash of hot sauce

Combine all ingredients in a 5 quart crockpot. Cook for 6 - 7 hours on low. Shred meat with fork and place mixture on buns.

Makes 12 sandwiches.

These recipes are very similar. I included them both because which one I make depends on what ingredients I have available.

-Ruth

Sloppy Joe Sandwiches

3 cloves garlic, minced
1/2 cup chopped onion
1 tsp. olive oil

Sauté the garlic and onion in the oil for 1 - 2 minutes.

1 lb. ground beef

Add the ground beef and brown. Drain.

2 tsp. Worcestershire sauce
2 Tbsp. brown sugar
1 tsp. mustard
1/2 cup ketchup
salt and pepper to taste
1/4 tsp. chili powder
dash of red pepper, optional
dash of cumin, optional

Add the next 8 ingredients. Simmer and stir until seasonings are well blended.

1 - 2 Tbsp. quick oatmeal, to
   thicken, optional

Simmer for 10 - 15 minutes, adding the oats if sandwich mixture is too juicy.

4 - 6 sandwich rolls

Spoon mixture over the rolls and serve immediately.

Options:
*Add 2 slices cooked, crumbled bacon prior to simmering.

*Place a slice of Colby cheese in each sandwich.

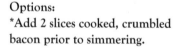

Ruth

Club Sandwich

3 slices white or wheat bread,
    thinly sliced

Lightly toast bread.

mayonnaise
mustard

*Add mayonnaise and mustard to
one side of each slice, to taste.*

3 - 4 slices deli meat of choice
    -turkey
    -ham
    -roast beef
    -chicken
1 - 2 slices cheese of choice
    -American
    -Muenster
    -Provolone
    -Swiss
    -Colby

*Layer the meat and cheese between
two of the bread slices.*

2 - 3 slices bacon, cooked
lettuce
1 - 2 thin tomato slices

*Top the remaining slice of bread
with the bacon, lettuce and tomato
slices.*
*Place this layer on top of the meat
and cheese 'sandwich' and cut in
half diagonally. Secure with a
toothpick.*

Serves 1.

-Ruth

Crab Cakes

8 saltine crackers, crushed
1/8 tsp. Old Bay seasoning
1/8 tsp. onion powder
1/8 tsp. black pepper

Mix saltines and seasonings together. (Add more or less of seasonings to taste.)

1 lb. crab meat
1/4 tsp. parsley

Add the crab meat and parsley to the saltine mixture.

1 egg
2 Tbsp. mayonnaise
2 Tbsp. Dijon mustard

Mix egg, mayonnaise and mustard together in a separate bowl. Add crab mixture, stirring gently.

6 sandwich rolls
lettuce
tomato slices
mayonnaise

Shape into patties and fry on buttered skillet. Serve warm on buns with lettuce, tomato and mayonnaise.

Makes 6 sandwiches.

-Ruth

Philly Cheese Steak Sandwiches

1 lb. beef sirloin steak, cut into
    thin strips
1 medium green pepper, sliced
    thin strips
1 medium onion, sliced into
    thin strips
2 Tbsp. steak sauce
2 Tbsp. water
1 tsp. garlic
salt and pepper, to taste

4 sub sandwich rolls
4 slices American or Swiss cheese

Place all ingredients into a casserole dish, cover and bake for 1 1/2 hours at 325°.

Divide mixture evenly between sandwich rolls. Place cheese slice over beef mixture. (Sometimes I will toast the sandwich rolls to keep it from soaking into the bread as quickly).

-Marti

Cucumber and Radish Tea Sandwiches

Bread slices, can be white or wheat , as many slices as desired sandwiches

Salad dressing
Ranch dressing mix

Cucumbers
Radishes

Paprika
Dill weed

These sandwiches are a nice 'extra' to serve at a luncheon shower or tea.

I use a cookie cutter to cut fancy shapes out of the bread slices, or you can simply remove the crusts and cut in half and then quarters diagonally. This can be done ahead and stored in a bread bag to maintain freshness.
Plan ahead how you want to cut the bread as this will make a difference how many slices you will need, if you use a large cutter you'll only get one sandwich per slice.

Combine the salad dressing and ranch mix according to package directions. Set aside.

Wash the vegetables and pat dry. Take a fork and rake it down the sides of the cucumber, pressing hard enough to leave definite marks. (This creates a pretty flower design.) Slice the radishes and cucumbers into thin slices.
Just prior to serving, spread a thin layer of the ranch dressing over the bread and top with the cucumber and radish slices. If you have larger pieces of bread, you may need three slices of radish slightly overlapping each other.
Sprinkle the paprika over the cucumber sandwiches and dill weed over the radish sandwiches.

-Carolyn

Almond Chicken Salad

2 1/2 cups chicken, cooked and
    cubed
1 1/2 cups mayonnaise
1/4 tsp. pepper
1/2 tsp. salt
1 tsp. chicken stock seasoning
2 Tbsp. chopped almonds
2 Tbsp. chopped onions - opt.
1/2 cup chopped celery
2 Tbsp. peppercorn Ranch
    dressing

Mix all ingredients with fork. Chill. Serve this mixture between two slices of bread, croissants, or small sandwich rolls.
You can also use miniature dinner rolls, slicing part way down through the center from top of roll and stuff with salad. Place a small sprig of washed and dried parsley on top.

We've used this recipe for many weddings and bridal showers that we've catered. It has a very unique taste.

-Mom

Tuna Salad

1 (6 oz.) can tuna, drained
1 egg, hard-boiled, chopped
3 Tbsp. onion, chopped
3 Tbsp. celery, chopped
1 tsp. lemon juice
1/4 cup salad dressing
1/8 tsp. celery seed
1 tsp. prepared mustard
salt to taste

Combine all ingredients and gently mix with fork until seasonings are well blended.
Chill.

Spread over bread slices or with crackers.

For a party or shower food, use cookie cutters to cut bread, some white and some wheat. Spread filling over one kind of bread and top with the other. Alternate on your serving plate.

-Ruth

Egg Salad Sandwiches

4 eggs, hard-boiled and chopped
3 Tbsp. diced celery
3 Tbsp. chopped onion, optional
1/4 cup salad dressing
1 tsp. mustard
1/4 tsp. celery seed
salt to taste

Combine all ingredients and stir gently with a fork till thoroughly mixed.

Chill.

See tuna salad sandwich recipe on page 69 for serving ideas.

-Carolyn

Deviled Eggs

6 eggs, hard-boiled and cooled

Cut eggs in half.
Remove yolks and place in small mixing bowl. Mash with fork until finely crumbled.

6 Tbsp. mayonnaise
1/2 tsp. mustard
1/4 tsp. celery seed
dash of salt and pepper
dash of dill seasoning mix,
   optional

dill weed

Add remaining ingredients and mix well.
Use a decorator icing bag with a large tip. Fill with the yolk mixture and refill the egg white shells.

Sprinkle dill weed over tops of filled eggs.

-Ruth

Skillet Chicken Salad

3 Tbsp. butter
3 large boneless, skinless chicken
   breasts, cut in 3"x1/2"
   strips
1/4 tsp. salt
1/4 tsp. pepper

In a 10-inch skillet, melt butter. Stir in chicken, salt and pepper. Cook over medium heat until chicken is browned and tender. Remove from heat.

1/4 cup chopped celery
1/4 cup chopped onions
1/4 cup chopped fresh parsley
1/3 cup sour cream
1/3 cup mayonnaise
1 Tbsp. country-style Dijon
   mustard
1 Tbsp. lemon juice

Stir in next 7 ingredients.

8 large lettuce leaves
1 cup cherry tomato halves

On platter or four individual salad plates, arrange the lettuce leaves, place chicken salad on platter over lettuce or divide evenly among the four plates. Arrange cherry tomatoes around salad.
Delicious served with fresh fruit for a luncheon.

Serves 4.

-Ruth

Pasta Salad

12 oz. rotini pasta

Cook pasta according to package directions. Drain and set aside.

1 1/2 cups Italian dressing
1/2 cup water
2/3 cup sugar
2 tsp. Italian seasoning
dash of salt

Place the next 5 ingredients into a food processor or blender and blend for 2 - 3 minutes. Pour over the pasta, mix well.

3/4 cup diced or finely chopped
   carrots*
1/2 cup chopped green peppers*
1/2 cup chopped onion*
pepperoni slices, cut in quarters,
   to taste*

Add the chopped carrots, peppers, onions and pepperoni to pasta and mix well.
Chill.

*all vegetables and pepperoni are optional and can be omitted or substituted.

Stir again before serving.

'Tis an ill cook that
cannot lick his own
fingers.
- William Shakespeare

-Carolyn

Macaroni Salad

1 box (16 oz.) elbow macaroni

Cook macaroni according to directions on package. Drain.

4 eggs, hard-boiled and chopped
1 medium onion, chopped
3 carrots, diced
2 stalks celery, diced
4 oz. Colby or American cheese,
    cut into small cubes

Add the next 5 ingredients.

Dressing:
2 1/4 cups salad dressing
1 cup sugar
3 Tbsp. mustard
1 tsp. vinegar
2/3 cup milk

Combine all the dressing ingredients and blend. Pour over the pasta mixture and stir until well blended. Chill.
Stir again just prior to serving. Garnish with parsley and tomato wedges.

-Carolyn

Potato Salad

6 cups cooked potatoes, diced
    or shredded
4 hard-boiled eggs, chopped
3/4 cup chopped celery
1/4 cup chopped onion

Mix all ingredients together.

Dressing:
3/4 cup sugar
1 cup salad dressing
2 Tbsp. vinegar
1 Tbsp. prepared mustard
1/2 tsp. salt
1/4 tsp. celery seed

Mix all ingredients together and add to the above mixture. Chill and serve.

-Ruth

Tossed Salad

It is important to start your salad with crisp, fresh lettuce that is rinsed and dried thoroughly. There are many different greens you may use in your salad; here are a few of our favorite salad fixins'.

Salad Greens:
iceberg
romaine
leafy red or green
mixed salad greens (mesculin)

Toppings:
carrots
celery
tomatoes
onions
radishes
peppers
mushrooms
alfalfa sprouts
boiled eggs

croutons
shredded cheddar
parmesan cheese
broccoli
cauliflower
cottage cheese
sunflower seeds
bacon
chopped chives

Choose your family's favorite toppings and toss gently with the greens.
Just before serving, top with your favorite dressing and enjoy!

Homemade Salad Croutons

Cube 5 - 6 slices of bread.

Melt 1/4 cup butter in the microwave,
Add 1/2 tsp. Italian seasoning to the melted butter and mix well.
Place the cubed bread in the butter mixture and toss until well coated.
Place in the microwave on high for 1 minute - remove, stir and return to microwave for another 2 minutes, or until moisture seems to be absorbed. (They will become crispy as they cool.)
Spread out on paper towels until cooled. Store in sealed container till ready to use.

Greek Salad Dressing

6 Tbsp. olive oil
2 Tbsp. vinegar
2 tsp. country Dijon mustard
2 tsp. oregano
pinch of salt and pepper

Mix and shake well before using.

-Bethany's favorite

Confetti Slaw

1/2 - 3/4 head of cabbage
1 medium carrot, grated
1 Tbsp. chopped onion
2 tsp. finely chopped green
    pepper, optional

Dressing:
1/2 cup salad dressing
1/4 cup sugar
1/4 tsp. prepared mustard
dash of celery salt
1/4 cup milk

Coarsely chop the cabbage and carrot in food processor. Add the onion and pepper to the cabbage mixture.

Stir all dressing ingredients until smooth and sugar dissolves. Pour over cabbage mixture, stir until well coated. Refrigerate until ready to serve.

Serves 6.

We enjoy this over hot dogs in buns to create 'slaw dogs', as well as a summer side dish.

-Carolyn

Coleslaw Dressing

2 cups salad dressing
1 cup sugar
1 tsp. prepared mustard
1/4 cup vinegar
1/4 cup evaporated milk
1/2 tsp. celery seed

Beat together until creamy. Store in refrigerator.

Approximately enough for 1 - 1 1/2 head of grated cabbage.

I keep this stored in my refrigerator up to 1 week and use small amounts as needed for meals.

-Ruth

Broccoli-Cauliflower Salad

2 large bunches broccoli
1 large head cauliflower

Cut broccoli and cauliflower into bite-sized pieces.

1 Tbsp. chopped onions
3 Tbsp. bacon bits
6 hard-boiled eggs, chopped - optional
1 tomato cubed -optional

Add the next 4 ingredients to the vegetables.

2 cups dressing recipe (see below)

Add dressing, stirring gently until mixed.

1 1/2 cups shredded cheddar cheese

Top with shredded cheese.

Serves 12 - 15.

Dressing:
2 cups mayonnaise
2/3 cup sugar
2 Tbsp. vinegar
2 tsp. prepared mustard
1/4 cup milk
1 tsp. salt

Mix all ingredients with wire whisk until smooth; place in a covered container and keep refrigerated.

Makes 2 cups.

I use this dressing for the Broccoli-Cauliflower salad as well as potato salad and cole slaw.

-Mom

Cranberry Jello Salad

2 (3 oz.) boxes raspberry jello
2 cups boiling water

Mix jello and boiling water together
and stir until jello is dissolved.

1 (16 oz.) can cranberry sauce

Add the cranberry sauce and stir
until dissolved and separated.

2 cups grated apples
1 (20 oz.) can crushed pineapple,
   undrained

Add apples and pineapple. Pour
into a large mold and refrigerate
until set.

A tasty and attractive way to serve this salad is to fill the
center of the unmolded jello with cottage cheese.

-Kathleen

Moon Cheese Salad

1 (3 oz.) box lime gelatin
1 cup boiling water

Mix gelatin with boiling water,
stirring till dissolved.

1 cup pineapple juice
8 oz. crushed pineapple
1 cup sour cream
1 cup cottage cheese

Add remaining ingredients. Pour
into serving dish, chill and serve.

Bethany introduced this recipe to us when she made it for
a math assignment in fourth grade.

-Ruth

Frosted Raspberry Squares

2 (3 oz.) boxes of raspberry
    gelatin
2 cups boiling water

In a large bowl dissolve gelatin in boiling water.

12 oz. package fresh or frozen
    raspberries, thawed
1 cup sugar
2/3 cup orange juice
1 (20 oz.) can crushed pineapple,
    undrained
1 tsp. grated orange peel

Stir raspberries and remaining ingredients into the dissolved gelatin. Pour into a 9"x13" pan. Cover and refrigerate until firm, 6 hrs. or overnight.

Topping:
3 oz. cream cheese, softened
1 cup whipping cream
2 Tbsp. sugar
1 tsp. vanilla
1 cup miniature marshmallows

Garnish options:
lettuce
mint leaves
sugared raspberries
orange slices

In a small mixing bowl beat cream cheese until light and fluffy. Add whipping cream, beat at low speed until mixed, increase speed to high until stiff peaks form. Stir in sugar and vanilla. By hand fold in marshmallows. Spread over the raspberry gelatin. Refrigerate at least one hour. Cut into squares, place on individual plates, on bed of lettuce if desired. Garnish with sugared raspberries and mint leaves or orange slices and mint leaves.

-Ruth

We may live without poetry,
music and art;
We may live without conscience
and live without heart;
We may live without friends;
We may live without books;
But civilized man cannot
live without cooks.

-Owen Meredith

Main
Dishes

MAIN DISHES

Chicken Breasts Supreme

6 boneless chicken breast halves

Flatten chicken to 1/4" thickness using a meat mallet.

6 deli ham slices
6 slices Swiss cheese

Fold cheese slices into quarters. Wrap a slice of ham around each folded slice of cheese and place in center of chicken breast.
Fold or roll the chicken breast securely around the ham and secure with toothpicks.

1/2 cup (1 stick) butter, melted

Dip chicken rolls into the melted butter.

Bread Crumb mixture:
1 cup bread crumbs
1 tsp. paprika
1/2 tsp. salt
1/2 tsp. pepper
1/4 tsp. poultry seasoning
1/2 tsp. Mrs. Dash

Roll buttered breast in the bread crumb mixture.

8 oz. sour cream
1 - 10 3/4 oz. can cream of
    chicken or celery soup

Mix sour cream and soup together. Pour into a baking dish and place stuffed breasts on top of the mixture.
Cover and bake at 350° for 45 minutes to 1 hour, or until juices run clear.

Serves 6.

-Ruth

Chicken Bundles

This recipe must be prepared ahead of time and requires marinating. The end result is worth the extra time and planning!

6 large boneless, skinless chicken breast halves

Flatten chicken to 1/4" thickness using a meat mallet. Set aside.

1/2 cup molasses
1/4 cup olive oil
1/4 cup lemon juice
1/4 cup soy sauce
2 Tbsp. Worcestershire sauce
1/2 tsp. ground ginger
1/4 tsp. garlic powder

Combine molasses and the next 6 ingredients, stir until spices are well blended. Pour mixture over the chicken; marinate in refrigerator for 4 - 6 hours.

1/4 cup butter
3/4 lb. fresh mushrooms, sliced
1/2 cup onions, chopped
1/2 tsp. salt
1/4 tsp. pepper

Melt the butter in a large skillet. Add the mushrooms, onions, salt and pepper. Sauté over medium heat until vegetables are tender, stirring frequently.
Remove chicken from the marinade. Pour marinade into a small saucepan; bring to a boil and remove from heat. Reserve.

12 slices bacon

cooked rice

fresh parsley

For each chicken bundle; place 2 slices bacon in a crisscross pattern on a flat surface. Place the chicken in center of the bacon slices. Top with 3 Tbsp. mushroom mixture. Fold sides and ends of chicken breasts over the mushroom mixture to make a square shaped pouch. Pull bacon around chicken and tie ends together, secure with wooden picks. Place the bundles on the grill; cook over low heat for 30 - 40 minutes or until done, turning and basting with the reserved marinade every 15 minutes.

This is nice served over rice and garnished with parsley.

Serves 6.

-Ruth

Chicken Cacciatore

6 skinless, boneless chicken breasts

Place chicken breasts in a 2 quart baking dish.

1 (14 1/2 oz.) can stewed tomatoes
1 (8 oz.) can tomato juice
1 (4 oz.) can mushrooms, optional
1 medium onion, sliced
1 medium green pepper, sliced
2 tsp. oregano leaves
1/2 tsp. garlic powder

Mix these ingredients together and pour over the chicken breasts. Bake at 350° for 45 minutes.

This is delicious served over rice or toast and it's Ben's favorite leftover dish!

-Marti

Italian Chicken Spaghetti

4 boneless, chicken breasts

1 medium green pepper, chopped
1 medium onion, chopped
1 jar (24 oz.) spaghetti sauce

8 oz. spaghetti noodles, cooked according to directions on box.

Cut chicken breasts into 1/2" to 1" pieces. Place in skillet, or baking dish. Add remaining ingredients and simmer in skillet until chicken is tender, about 30 minutes. Or bake at 350° for about 45 minutes.

Serve over noodles.

-Marti

Chicken with Zucchini and Garlic Sauce

1/4 cup butter
6 boneless chicken breast halves,
    cut in half
salt and pepper to taste
1/4 tsp. Mrs. Dash, optional

Melt the butter in a large skillet. Add the chicken and seasonings; cook over medium heat, until chicken is browned and fork tender.

3 cups sliced zucchini
1/3 cup chopped onions or
    sliced green onions

Add the zucchini and onions; continue cooking, stirring gently until zucchini is crisp-tender.

Garlic Cream:
2 Tbsp. butter
1 tsp. minced fresh garlic
3 Tbsp. flour
3 oz. cream cheese
1 - 10 3/4 oz. can chicken broth
1/2 tsp. pepper

Meanwhile, melt butter in a 2 quart saucepan; add garlic and cook for 1 minute. Add flour; cooking and stirring until smooth and bubbly. Add cream cheese and broth, stirring until sauce is thickened. Add pepper.

cooked rice

Place rice on a platter; arrange chicken and zucchini pieces on top of rice, top with garlic cream sauce.

Serves 6.

-Ruth

Stir-fry Chicken and Squash with Pasta

10 oz. Bow Tie or Seashell pasta,
    or any pasta you like

Cook pasta according to package
directions. Drain.

1 Tbsp. butter
1 cup whipping cream
1 cup milk
2 cups shredded cheddar cheese
1/4 tsp. salt

Meanwhile, heat the cream, milk
and butter in a 2-quart saucepan
until butter melts. Add the cheese
and salt; cook and stir until smooth.
Stir into the drained pasta, cover
and keep warm.

1/3 cup chopped onion
1 garlic clove, minced
3 Tbsp. cooking oil
3 cups yellow squash, julienned
3 cups zucchini, julienned
1 tsp. salt
1/4 tsp. pepper

In a skillet over medium heat, sauté
the onion and garlic in oil till crisp-
tender. Add squash; cook until
tender. add salt and pepper.
Remove and keep warm.

2 Tbsp. cooking oil
4 - 5 boneless, skinless chicken
    breasts, cut into 1/2"x2"
    strips
1/4 tsp. salt
2 tsp. soy sauce
1/4 tsp. basil
1/4 tsp. rosemary
1/4 tsp. thyme
1/4 tsp. garlic salt

In same skillet, cook chicken in oil
with seasonings until juices run
clear.
To serve, place pasta on serving
platter; top with the squash and
then the chicken.

Makes 6 - 8 servings.

-Carolyn

Garlic Broiled Chicken

4 bone-in chicken breast halves

Place on a baking sheet.

1/4 cup butter (no substitutes), melted
1/4 tsp. pepper
3 Tbsp. minced fresh garlic
1/2 tsp. basil
1/4 cup soy sauce
1/4 cup chopped parsley

Combine these ingredients and pour over chicken. Bake at 350°, turning and brushing with butter mixture every 10 minutes. Bake for 45 - 50 minutes or until fork tender and juices run clear. Then broil until tops are browned.

cooked rice

Serve with rice.

Serves 4.

-Marti

Grilled Chicken Breasts

4 Tbsp. butter, melted
1/4 cup olive oil
1 Tbsp. soy sauce
1/2 tsp. salt
1/4 tsp. pepper
1/2 tsp. Mrs. Dash, original
1/4 tsp. chopped chives
1/4 tsp. chopped parsley

Combine all ingredients.

Pour marinade over the chicken and set in refrigerator at least 1 hour. Grill until chicken is tender and juices run clear.

4 - 6 boneless chicken breasts

-Ruth

Chicken Marinade

3/4 cup vegetable oil
1/4 cup melted butter
1/4 cup lemon juice
1 Tbsp. mustard
2 Tbsp. brown sugar
1 Tbsp. salt
1/2 tsp. red pepper
2 tsp. onion salt
1/2 tsp. Worcestershire sauce
1/4 cup ketchup

Combine all ingredients, mix well.

This will marinate 2 cut up chickens. Marinate for 2 - 3 hours or overnight.

Can be stored in refrigerator in a covered container until ready to use.

-Ruth

Steak Marinade

This marinade works well with any steak, whether you want to grill, bake or broil them. One recipe is enough for 2 - 3 lbs. of meat.

1 1/2 cups beef broth
3/4 cup soy sauce
1/4 cup Worcestershire sauce
1 medium onion, chopped
1 medium pepper, chopped
2 garlic cloves, minced
2 Tbsp. vinegar
2 Tbsp. lemon juice
2 tsp. dried parsley flakes
1 tsp. dried thyme
1 tsp. Italian seasoning
1 tsp. pepper
2 Tbsp. Dijon mustard

Combine all ingredients into a mixing bowl and mix well; pour over steaks.
Cover and refrigerate overnight.
Remove meat and discard marinade.
Grill or bake to desired doneness.

-Marti

Backyard Barbecue

Outdoor meals are a relaxing and enjoyable way to serve your guests. Here are some of our favorite grilling and barbecue ideas.

Kabobs....

Chicken - Cut boneless chicken breasts into 1" pieces, marinate for 2 - 3 hours or overnight. For marinade recipes see pages 88 & 89 or simply use Italian dressing or your favorite pre-mixed marinade available at your supermarket. Chicken cut into small pieces does not take long to finish cooking on the grill, so if you're adding vegetable like potatoes, carrots or corn on the cob, we like to par-boil them for 1 - 2 minutes before placing them on the skewer.

Beef - Cut into 1" pieces and marinate for 6 - 8 hours or overnight. (Use your favorite marinade recipe.) If your family enjoys rare meat you will need to partially cook the vegetables before placing them on the skewer. If you like the meat well done, it may be a good idea to partially grill or bake the steaks before placing on the skewer.

Shrimp or Sausage - are other meat options.

Vegetables you can use with your kabobs...

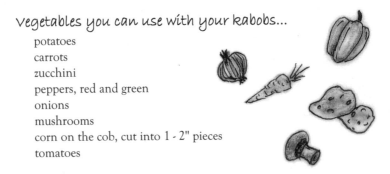

potatoes
carrots
zucchini
peppers, red and green
onions
mushrooms
corn on the cob, cut into 1 - 2" pieces
tomatoes

Melt butter, add seasonings of your choice, (We like salt and pepper, and Mrs. Dash seasoning). Dip the vegetables into this mixture before placing them on the skewers.

If you are using wooden skewers, soak them in warm water at least 30 minutes prior to using to keep them from burning on the grill.

Enjoy your meal with a tossed salad and fresh fruit.

Beef Roast... a 1 1/2" - 2" thick roast is a nice size to grill. Marinate for 6 - 8 hours or overnight, again using your favorite marinade recipe. An option for more flavor: take a sharp knife and poke holes into the roast approximately 1" apart and stuff each one with peeled garlic buds, before placing in marinade. Place on pre-heated grill on low heat, grilling each side 10 - 15 minutes or until desired doneness. Since we do not enjoy rare meat, we usually remove the roast from the grill after 30 minutes; slice it thinly and place the slices on a heavy duty aluminum foil, wrap and return to grill till desired doneness.

Potato Pouches... Cut unpeeled and washed new potatoes into 1" - 2" pieces and parboil. Place onto pieces of heavy duty aluminum foil (one pouch per person). Sprinkle with seasonings of your choice, (we like salt, pepper, Mrs. Dash or Nature's Seasons). Add onion slices or chopped onions. Dot with butter and wrap tightly. Place on medium hot grill for approximately 20 minutes, 10 minutes per side. If you peek in to check doneness, be careful of a steam burn!

Grilled Vegetables... Use any combination of the vegetables mentioned on page 90. Slice or cut into bite sized pieces, dip into melted butter and seasonings of your choice. Place directly on the grill using a grill screen, or pot designed to be used on a grill, or use an aluminum foil pouch. Grill for 5 - 10 minutes or until desired doneness.

A complete meal idea... Tear off large pieces of heavy duty aluminum foil, one for each person you are serving, in the center of the foil place a cabbage leaf. Then add a seasoned raw hamburger patty, a few cut new potatoes or potato slices, baby carrots, chopped or sliced onions, a few butter pats and seasonings or fresh herbs from your garden. Seal the foil and place on a hot grill for 25 - 35 minutes. This is an easy, complete meal, served with iced tea, of course!

Other side dish ideas...

Tossed Salad - see page 74 & 75
Potato Salad - see page 73
Pasta Salad - see pages 72 & 73
Cole Slaw - see page 76
Calico Beans - see page 124
Summer Bean Casserole - see page 125

Lemon Pepper Chicken

2 cups all-purpose flour
4 tsp. lemon pepper seasoning
1 tsp. garlic powder
4 tsp. parsley flakes
2 tsp. salt
1 tsp. black pepper
Accent

8 skinless, boneless chicken
    breasts
4 Tbsp. butter flavored Crisco

Combine the flour and seasonings, mixing well.

Roll the chicken breasts in the above seasoning mixture. Fry in the Crisco, till golden brown. Sprinkle with Accent and place in baking dish. Bake at 325° for 1 hour. Place on serving dish and garnish with parsley and lemon wedges.

-Mom

Chicken Rice Casserole

This recipe is easy and quick and a fun way to use up leftover rice or chicken. Curry is the seasoning that gives its unique flavor.

1/4 cup onion, chopped
1/2 cup celery, chopped
1/4 cup butter

1 cup chicken broth
1 cup milk
1 (10 3/4 oz.) can cream of
    chicken soup

2 cups cooked chicken, diced
2 cups cooked rice
1 1/2 tsp. salt
1/2 tsp. pepper
1 1/2 tsp. curry powder

Sauté onions and celery in melted butter.

Add the broth, milk and soup to the above mixture; heat thoroughly.

Add all these ingredients to the broth mixture, mixing well.

Pour into a 9"x13" baking dish. Bake at 325° for 30 - 40 minutes.

-Ruth

Baked Chicken with Crab

8 boneless chicken breast halves

Flatten chicken breasts to 1/4" thickness.

3 Tbsp. butter
1/4 cup flour
1 cup milk
1 cup chicken broth
2 oz. cream cheese

Melt the butter in a heavy saucepan, add flour stirring until smooth. Gradually add the milk and broth. Cook until thick and bubbly. Add cream cheese and stir until melted. Add salt and pepper to taste. Set aside.

1 Tbsp. butter
1/8 cup chopped onion

In large skillet sauté onion in butter until tender. Remove from heat. Add the crabmeat and remaining ingredients. Stir. Add 2 Tbsp. of the cream cheese mixture, mix well.

1 (6 oz.) can crabmeat, drained
10 saltine crackers, crushed
2 Tbsp. fresh parsley
1/2 tsp. salt
1/2 tsp. pepper
1/2 tsp. Old Bay seasoning

Optional: Sprinkle with paprika and parsley for garnish before serving.

Serves 8.

Top each chicken breast with 1/8 cup of the crabmeat mixture. Fold long sides of chicken over the crabmeat and place chicken rolls seams down in a 9"x13" baking dish. (Chicken may be secured with toothpicks before placing in pan.) Top with remaining cream cheese sauce. Cover and bake at 350° for 1 hour or until juices from chicken run clear.

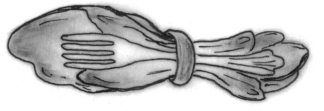

-Ruth

Swiss Chicken Casserole

6 skinless, boneless chicken
   breasts
6 (4"x4") slices Swiss cheese

1 (10 3/4 oz.) can cream of
   chicken soup
1/4 cup milk

2 cups herb-seasoned stuffing
   mix
1/4 cup butter, melted

*Arrange chicken breasts in a lightly
greased baking dish. Top with the
cheese slices.*

*Combine the soup and milk, spoon
over the chicken.*

*Sprinkle the stuffing mix over the
sauce and chicken and then drizzle
with the melted butter.*

*Cover and bake at 350° for
50 - 60 minutes.*

The Quick Version

**Chicken breasts can be
pre-cooked; just add
remaining ingredients as
listed and bake just until
heated all through.**

-Hannah

Chicken Stir-Fry

1 Tbsp. cooking oil
2 - 3 cloves garlic, minced
1/2 cup onion, chopped
4 boneless chicken breasts, cut
    into 1 1/2" pieces

In a large skillet, sauté the onion &
garlic in oil.
Add the chicken pieces & cook until
tender.

1 cup sliced carrots
1 cup sliced celery
1 cup broccoli, cut into small
    pieces
1/4 cup sliced or chopped green
    pepper
1/4 head of cabbage, chopped,
    optional

Add the vegetables & simmer for 3 -
5 minutes; stirring frequently.

1 cup water
1/4 - 1/2 cup soy sauce
salt and pepper to taste
1/4 tsp. Mrs. Dash, original
1/4 cup corn starch

Cooked rice

Combine water with the next 4
ingredients; pour over meat and
vegetable mixture, continue to
simmer until vegetables are tender,
another 5 - 8 minutes.

Serve over cooked rice.

Optional addition:

1 1/2 pounds small salad
*   shrimp - cooked and*
*   de-veined*
Add a few minutes before
recipe is ready to serve, just
long enough to heat shrimp.

-Ruth

Chicken Pie

3 - 4 large boneless chicken
    breasts
water
1 bay leaf
salt & pepper

*Cover the chicken breasts and
seasonings with water and boil until
chicken is tender. Set aside.*

Crust:
2 cups flour
3 tsp. baking powder
1 tsp. salt
1/2 cup shortening
3/4 cup milk

*Cut shortening into the dry
ingredients using a pastry blender or
food processor until it forms coarse
crumbles. Stir in milk until dough
leaves the sides of bowl.*
*Turn dough onto floured surface,
divide evenly into 2 parts and roll
both parts out to fit into a 9" deep
dish pie pan. Place one round into
the pie pan and press down into
pan.*

1 quart chicken stock
flour

*Remove the chicken from the stock
and dice into 1" pieces. Make a
gravy from the stock and flour and
pour approximately 1 cup over the
chicken pieces. Place the chicken
and gravy mixture into pie shell,
cover with remaining dough round.
Press edges together, trim excess then
crimp edges. Make several slits with
knife across top of pie for vents.
Bake at 350° for 30 minutes. Serve
with the remaining gravy.*

*If you use the optional vegetables
cook them until tender, then add to
the chicken and gravy mixture.*

Ruth's Chicken-Vegetable Pot Pie:

1 cup diced potatoes
1 cup diced carrots
1/2 cup diced celery
2 Tbsp. chopped onion
(If you add all the above
vegetables, you may
want to use less chicken.)

This recipe was given to me by Virginia Cooper, who I met
through the volunteer lunch program at Bethany's school. She is
one of the most organized persons I have ever met and I've
enjoyed our friendship.

-Ruth

Cheesy Asparagus and Chicken Casserole

4 cups bread cubes
1 cup shredded cheddar cheese
1/4 cup butter, melted

Toss the bread cubes with the cheese and butter.
Place 1/2 of bread cubes into a 2 quart baking dish.

2 cups asparagus pieces, cooked

Spread drained asparagus over the bread cubes.

White Sauce:
1/4 cup butter
1/3 cup flour
1 tsp. salt
1/4 tsp. seasoned salt
1/4 tsp. pepper
2 cups milk or broth

Melt the butter; add flour and seasonings. Add the milk (or broth) slowly and cook until thickened.

2 cups cooked and diced chicken

Fold the chicken pieces into the sauce.
Pour over the asparagus. Sprinkle with remaining bread cubes.

Bake uncovered at 350° for 30 minutes or until bread is golden brown and casserole is bubbly.

-Kathleen

Thanksgiving Stuffing

16 cups bread cubes
pepper
seasoned salt
garlic powder
oregano

2 cups chopped celery
2 cups diced carrots
2 Tbsp. butter

1 cup chopped onion
4 cups diced, cooked potatoes
6 cups chicken or turkey,
  cooked and cut up
1/2 tsp. celery salt
1 tsp. poultry seasoning
1 tsp. thyme leaves
3 tsp. parsley flakes
salt and pepper to taste

1 cup butter, melted
1 cup water
4 1/2 cups chicken or turkey
  broth
4 Tbsp. chicken gravy base*

1 1/2 cups milk
3 Tbsp. cornstarch

*This can be the chicken bouillon
or base found in any grocery
store, but I use and prefer the
rich chicken gravy seasoning
found at bulk food stores. It can
also be eliminated and more
poultry seasoning and salt can be
substituted.

Spread bread cubes out on two cookie
sheets and sprinkle lightly with the
seasonings. Bake at 250° until lightly
browned and crunchy.
Pour into a large mixing bowl.

Sauté the carrots and celery in butter
until slightly tender, being careful not
to overcook. Add to the bread crumbs.
Add onions, potatoes, meat and
seasonings; toss lightly until all
ingredients are well mixed.

Place the butter, water, broth and
soup base in medium saucepan and
bring to a boil.

Dissolve the cornstarch in the milk
and stir into boiling mixture, cooking
for 1 - 2 minutes. Set aside and let
cool till lukewarm. Pour the gravy
mixture over the bread mixture and
again toss gently until well coated.

Place into a large roasting pan or 2 -
9"x13" pans and bake for 1 1/2
hours, stirring half way through
baking time.

Serves approximately 20 - 24. If
you plan to stuff your turkey, be sure
to make extra filling.

-Carolyn

How to prepare a Thanksgiving Turkey

Remove giblet packet; thoroughly wash inside and
outside of turkey. Stuff the turkey cavities with
dressing, following recipe on page 98.

Place turkey breast side up in a large roasting pan. Add
1/2 - 1 cup water to bottom of pan.

Brush turkey with olive oil; sprinkle salt and pepper over
whole turkey. Leave uncovered; place in oven pre-heated to
325° . Approximate roasting times for stuffed turkey
are as follows:

8 - 10 pounds....5 - 6 hours

10 - 16 pounds....6 - 7 hours

18 - 25 pounds....7 1/2 - 8 1/2 hours

or bring to internal temperature of 180° - 185°.

Baste every 15 - 20 minutes with the meat drippings
during the whole baking time.

If the turkey seems to be browning too quickly, place a
foil tent loosely over the turkey.

Serve on a platter with fresh parsley.

Favorite Turkey-Rice Casserole

This is our family's favorite way to use left-over holiday turkey. If the turkey has been smoked, it is even better! This can be made any time of the year though, by using chicken in place of the turkey.

2 cups cooked white rice
4 - 6 cups turkey, cooked and
   diced
1 cup cheddar cheese, shredded
1 (4 oz.) can sliced mushrooms
1 (10 oz. bag) chopped, frozen
   broccoli, cooked

Spray 9"x13" baking dish with cooking spray. Spread the rice on the bottom, layer with the turkey, cheese, mushrooms and broccoli.

1 1/2 cup chicken broth
1 (10 3/4 oz.) can cream of
   mushroom soup

Pour broth over the layers then 'frost' with the mushroom soup.

1 cup shredded cheddar cheese

Sprinkle cheese evenly over the top of casserole. Bake at 350° for about 45 minutes or until heated through.

-Kathleen

Salisbury Steak

You'll need to plan ahead for this overnight recipe.

3 pounds ground beef
2 cups crushed saltine crackers
2 cups milk
3/4 cup chopped onion
1 Tbsp. salt
1/2 tsp. pepper

Mix the beef and next five ingredients together thoroughly. Place in a jelly roll pan. Refrigerate for approximately 6 hours or overnight.

1/2 cup butter

The next day, melt butter in a large skillet. Cut meat into squares; fry in butter on each side until lightly browned. Place in a casserole baking dish.

2 (10 3/4 oz.) cans beefy
   mushroom soup

Pour the soups over the steak squares; cover and bake at 350° for 1 hour.

Serves 12 - 14.

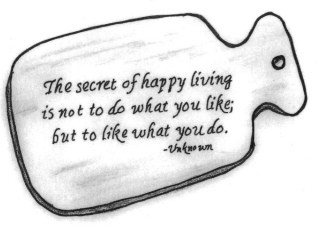

The secret of happy living is not to do what you like; but to like what you do.
-Unknown

-Mom

Tender Rump Roast

This roast is delicious served with mashed potatoes, gravy, green beans or corn with broccoli salad. I often make this when our family is together. For dessert we like apple pie and bob-andy pie.

8 pound rump roast

5 Tbsp. salt
5 Tbsp. black pepper
5 Tbsp. Accent
2 pkg. (dry) Lipton mushroom
   onion soup mix

Place 3 feet of tin foil on counter, center the roast on the foil and pat with the seasonings. Bring the foil around top and seal roast in. Place into large roasting pan and bake at 325° for 5 1/2 - 6 hours. Slice. Serves 15 - 18.

This roast can be made a day ahead and cooled in refrigerator over-night. Slice the next morning and wrap in foil and add 2 cups of broth retained from previous day before sealing with the foil. Warm in 300° oven for 1 hour.

Tasty Roast Gravy

3 cups broth from baked roast
3 cups water

Heat the broth and water to boiling.

3 Tbsp. clear jel or cornstarch
3/4 cup water

Mix the thickening with water until smooth, add to the boiling mixture slowly, stirring constantly with a wire whisk, until thickened.
May add more water for thinner gravy.
Add salt and other seasonings to taste.

-Mom

Meatloaf

2 pounds ground beef
1/3 cup chopped onion
1 Tbsp. Worcestershire sauce
1 1/2 tsp. salt
1/2 tsp. pepper
1 egg, lightly beaten with fork
1/4 cup ketchup
1/2 cup milk
1 cup quick oats
1/2 cup herb stuffing mix
1 pkg. Lipton onion soup mix

Place all ingredients into large mixing bowl and mix thoroughly. (I like to wear latex gloves and use my hands, since the mixture is thick and hard to mix with a spoon.) Pat into 2 loaf pans or into oblong shape in a 9"x13" pan.

Sauce:
1/4 cup water
1/3 cup ketchup
3 Tbsp. brown sugar
1 tsp. prepared mustard
1 Tbsp. Worcestershire sauce

Mix all the sauce ingredients together, stirring until sugar is dissolved. Pour evenly over the meatloaf.
Cover and bake at 350° for 1 hour.

Serves 8 - 10.

-Carolyn

Classic Lasagna

1 lb. ground sausage
1 Tbsp oil

In a large pot, brown the sausage in the oil.

1 (26 oz.) jar spaghetti sauce
1 (15 oz.) can tomato sauce
1 (14 1/2 oz.) can chicken broth
salt and pepper to taste

Add the next 4 ingredients to the sausage.

1 (15 oz.) carton ricotta cheese
2 cups cottage cheese
1/2 cup grated parmesan cheese
2 cups shredded mozzarella
cheese

In a large bowl, mix together the ricotta, cottage, parmesan and mozzarella cheeses.

Use 10"x15" baking dish for a large crowd, or 2 smaller dishes. (Freeze one prior to baking for later use. It tastes just as good as fresh.)

8 slices Provolone cheese
18 uncooked lasagna noodles

Layer 1/3 of tomato-meat mixture in baking dish, top with 1/2 of the uncooked noodles, 1/2 of the cheese mixture and 4 slices provolone cheese.

1 cup mozzarella cheese

Repeat layer and top with remaining 1/3 of tomato-meat mixture and remaining 1 cup of mozzarella cheese.
Cover and bake at 350° for 1 1/2 - 2 hours for large pan and 1 - 1 1/2 hours for the smaller pans. Uncover for last 15 minutes of baking time.

-Marti

Pizza Casserole

8 oz. package medium noodles

Cook noodles according to directions on package, drain and set aside.

1 pound ground beef
1/2 pound bulk sausage
1/2 cup chopped onion
1/4 cup chopped green pepper

While cooking the noodles, brown meats in skillet with the peppers and onions. Add to the noodles.

4 oz. canned mushrooms, drained
3 oz. pkg. pepperoni
1 (10 3/4 oz.) can cream of mushroom soup
16 oz. pizza sauce (2 cups)
1/2 tsp. garlic powder
1/2 tsp. oregano
1/2 tsp. thyme
1/4 tsp. celery seed
1 tsp. salt
dash of pepper
1/3 cup parmesan cheese

Add all the remaining ingredients except the mozzarella cheese to the meat and noodle mixture and stir together until the seasonings are thoroughly mixed.

Place into a 3 quart casserole baking dish or into a crock pot.

2 cups shredded mozzarella cheese

Top with the mozzarella cheese and bake at 350° for 40 minutes or until heated through; or it can also be heated in crock-pot on low heat for 3 hours or till heated through.

Serves 8.

This recipe freezes well. Since the recipe is enough for several meals for Jason & me, I usually place it into several meal-size containers and freeze prior to baking. Remove from freezer, partially thaw, and follow the baking instructions.

-Carolyn

Mexican Pie

Sour Cream Crust:
1/2 cup flour
1/2 tsp. baking powder
1/2 tsp. salt
1/4 cup butter flavored
    shortening
1/2 cup dairy sour cream
1 egg, beaten

Sift the dry ingredients together. Cut in the shortening as for biscuit dough. Stir in the sour cream and egg, just until well blended.
Spray a 9" glass or pottery pie pan with cooking spray and spread the dough evenly in the pan, pressing up the side of pan. Bake at 350° for 30 minutes or until lightly browned.

Meat Bean Topping:
1 lb. ground beef
2 Tbsp. Vidalia onions,
    chopped
1/2 tsp. salt
2 tsp. chili powder
1/4 tsp. hot sauce
1 (6 oz.) can tomato paste
1 (16 oz.) can chili hot beans or
    light kidney beans

While the crust is baking, brown the meat with the chopped onion. Drain and add the remaining ingredients. Simmer on low heat for 10 - 15 minutes, or until heated through and bubbly.

Spoon the meat mixture over the baked crust.

Toppings:
1/2 head lettuce, finely chopped
1 tomato, chopped
1/2 cup cheddar cheese, grated

salsa
sour cream or Ranch dressing

Top with lettuce, tomato and grated cheese. Cut into wedges and serve with the salsa, sour cream or ranch dressing.

Serves 6.

Our family enjoys this one-dish meal for a no fuss summer supper. Serve with brimming glasses of iced tea and finish off with a bowl of fresh melon

-Kathleen

Barbecued Spareribs

4 lbs. pork spareribs, cut into
    serving size pieces
1 medium onion, quartered
2 tsp. salt
1/4 tsp. pepper

Sauce:
1/2 cup vinegar
1/2 cup packed brown sugar
1/2 cup ketchup
1/4 cup Worcestershire sauce
1/4 cup chopped onion
1 Tbsp. lemon juice
1/2 tsp. dry mustard
1 - 2 garlic cloves, minced
dash of cayenne pepper

*Place ribs and onion into a large
kettle; sprinkle with salt and pepper.
Add enough water to cover ribs;
bring to a boil. Reduce heat, cover
and simmer for 1 1/2 hours or
until tender. Remove ribs from
water and set aside.*

*Meanwhile combine all sauce
ingredients in a medium saucepan.
Simmer, uncovered for 30 minutes
or until slightly thickened, stirring
occasionally. Dip ribs in the sauce
and place on the grill. Grill for 5
minutes on each side, brushing with
remaining sauce frequently.
(They can also be placed under
broiler for 5 minutes on each side.)*

Serves 4.

This is a good summertime
recipe, served with freshly
dug potatoes and carrots.
Just place washed vegetables
in a tin foil pouch; sprinkle
with salt, pepper, butter pats
and chopped fresh chives.
Close pouch tightly and place
on the grill on low for
approximately 30 minutes or
until vegetables are tender.

-Ruth

Honey-Gingered Pork Tenderloin

2 (3/4 lb.) pork tenderloins

Place into a 7"x11" baking dish.

1/4 cup honey
1/4 cup soy sauce
1/8 cup olive oil
2 Tbsp. brown sugar
1 Tbsp. ginger
1 Tbsp. minced garlic
1 Tbsp. ketchup
1/2 cup chopped onion
1/2 cup chopped green peppers
1/4 tsp. red pepper
1/4 tsp. black pepper
2 Tbsp. Dijon mustard

Combine all these ingredients, stirring until sugar is dissolved and well blended. Pour over the tenderloins; cover and marinate for 4 to 8 hours.

Bake at 350° for 1 hour, turning every 15 minutes.
To serve; slice tenderloins into thin slices and place on a serving platter, garnish with fresh parsley.

-Marti

Baked Fish

1 lb. fish fillets

Wash and dry fish fillets and place in a foil lined baking dish.

1/4 - 1/2 cup butter, melted
salt, to taste
lemon pepper, to taste
1/4 tsp. Old Bay seafood
  seasoning
1/4 tsp. dried chives
1/4 tsp. paprika

Mix all the remaining ingredients together. Pour over the fillets.

Bake at 350° for 20 - 25 minutes or until tender.

Our family enjoys mashed potatoes and a tossed salad with this easy fish recipe.

-Ruth

South Georgia Low Country Boil

2 gallons water
1/2 cup Old Bay seafood
   seasoning

Place the water and seasoning into a large stockpot. Bring to a boil.

8 onions, quartered
8 small new potatoes, whole
8 ears of corn, halved

Add these vegetables to the boiling water and cook for 10 minutes.

2 lbs. smoked sausage, cut into
   2" pieces.

Add to the vegetables and cook another 15 minutes.

3 lb. shrimp, unpeeled

Add the shrimp and cook until shrimp are pink and done.

Have table covered with a layer of newspaper; then cover with a heavy brown paper (the meat wrapping type).
Drain the water or if using a basket, lift out the basket and pour out the vegetables and meat onto the brown paper. Serve with melted butter and cocktail sauce.

This recipe came from my in-laws. My husband Ben does the cooking when we serve this and uses an outdoor gas cooker. It is ideal for an informal outdoor neighborhood or family get-together. Here in south Georgia we can enjoy it almost year round. I usually make a fresh vegetable tray and fresh melons to accompany this meal and for dessert, cheesecake and coffee is a good way to finish it off. My own family often asks for this meal when we are all together.

-Marti

Kitchen Terms

baking powder - a leavening agent combined of baking soda, cream of tarter, and cornstarch which, when combined with a liquid, releases carbon dioxide gas bubbles that cause dough or batter to rise.

baking soda - a leavening agent which, when combined with an acid such as buttermilk, yogurt, or molasses, produces carbon dioxide gas bubbles that cause a dough or batter to rise.

baste - to spoon or brush food as it cooks with melted butter, other fat, or drippings to keep food moist.

beat - to stir briskly in a circular motion; usually 100 strokes by hand equals about 1 minute with an electric mixer.

broil - to cook food directly under or above the heat source, such as in an oven or on a grill.

clear jel - a modified food starch derived from corn. It is more highly refined than corn starch and therefore gives better cooking results, especially when food is not used the first day. It is not sold in most grocery stores, but is usually found in bulk food stores. It is used like corn starch.

cream - to beat an ingredient or combination of ingredients until the mixture is soft and creamy, such as beating butter and sugar until the sugar is completely dissolved.

cut in - to distribute solid fat, such as shortening or butter, into dry ingredients, such as flour mixture, with a pastry blender or two knives until the mixture is like crumbs.

dash - a few sprinkles from a shaker.

dice - to cut food into small cubes.

dot - to scatter small bits of butter over a food or mixture so that it will melt evenly over the food as it bakes.

fold - to use a spatula to gently blend a lighter ingredient, such as beaten egg whites into a heavier mixture, using a gentle over and under motion.

julienne - food that has been cut into long, thin strips.

knead - to work a dough into a pliable mass by folding and stretching the dough with hands.

marinate - to soak food in a liquid, usually containing vinegar or other acid, along with spices. Improves flavor and tenderizes.

mince - to cut food into very small pieces.

parboil - to partially cook a food by boiling it in water briefly.

sauté - to cook food quickly over high heat in a small amount of fat.

stir-fry - a technique that requires a small amount of fat to fry food quickly over high heat, while stirring continuously.

stock - the richly flavored liquid in which meat or vegetables has cooked, used in soup or sauces.

whip - to beat ingredients rapidly at a high speed to incorporate air and increase volume.

Vegetables
and
Side Dishes

VEGETABLES AND SIDE DISHES

Herbed Potato Wedges

4 medium sized potatoes
1/2 cup butter, melted

Scrub potatoes and cut into eighths lengthwise. Place them into a 9"x13" baking dish. Pour the butter over the potatoes and stir until evenly coated, spreading into a single layer.

1/2 cup parmesan cheese
4 - 5 slices bacon, fried and crumbled
1/4 tsp. pepper
1 tsp. parsley flakes
1/2 tsp. thyme
1/2 tsp. garlic powder
1/2 tsp. seasoned salt

Sprinkle the cheese, bacon and seasonings over the potatoes. Bake at 350° for 20 - 25 minutes. Remove from oven and stir them until all wedges are well coated with the butter again. Return to oven and bake another 25 - 30 minutes or until tender.
Serves 4.

-Carolyn

Baked Parmesan Potatoes

1/3 cup butter

Preheat oven to 375° and melt the butter on a large cookie sheet.

6 large potatoes

Wash the potatoes, drain and cut into wedges.

1/4 cup flour
1/4 cup parmesan cheese
3/4 tsp. salt
1/8 tsp. pepper

Mix the flour, cheese, salt and pepper in a large plastic bag. Add the potato wedges and shake until well coated.

Serves 6.

Place the wedges in a single layer on the cookie sheet. Bake for 30 minutes; remove from oven and turn wedges. Return to oven for another 30 minutes or until potatoes are tender.

This recipe goes well with a backyard barbecue meal.

-Hannah

Cream Cheese Potatoes

5 lbs. potatoes, peeled and
    cubed

*Place the potatoes in a large
saucepan; cover with water and boil
until tender. Drain the water from
the potatoes; pour into large mixing
bowl and whip until light and
fluffy.*

2 tsp. salt
1 (8 oz.) pkg. cream cheese
4 Tbsp. butter
1/2 tsp. garlic salt
1/4 tsp. pepper
1 1/2 - 2 cups heavy cream

*Add the remaining ingredients and
mix well. Pour into a large baking
dish and bake at 325° for 1 - 1
1/2 hours.*

Optional:
2 Tbsp. butter, melted
paprika

Option:
*Pour melted butter over top of the
whipped potatoes and sprinkle with
paprika just before baking.*

Serves 12.

This recipe was given to me by Barbara
Schrock. She is a cousin to Jonas, and we have
often enjoyed her gift of hospitality. She is a
wonderful hostess and often opens her home to
guests, no matter how large the crowd is.

-Ruth

Mashed Potatoes

These potatoes stay creamy and can be made a day ahead!

10 lb. (or 25 medium sized) potatoes

Peel and cube the potatoes, placing in an 8 quart kettle, cover with water and boil until potatoes are soft.

Drain the potatoes and mash until smooth.

1 1/2 tsp. salt
1/2 cup butter
1 cup sour cream
3/4 cup milk, approx.

Add the remaining ingredients and blend with mixer until smooth and creamy. You may need to add more milk, depending on the consistency of your potatoes.

Variation:
For a cheesy version, you may substitute the sour cream for 1 cup of melted Velveeta cheese.

If you want to serve these potatoes immediately after whipping them, it is a good idea to warm the milk and butter in a saucepan or microwave prior to adding to the potatoes. I sometimes make these the day before, refrigerate overnight, place in crockpot the next day. Heat on the low setting for 2 hours, stirring every 1/2 hour.

Serves approx. 20.

I usually make these potatoes when our family comes home. It's a special treat for all my mashed potato lovers!

-Mom

Twice Baked Potatoes

5 - 6 baking potatoes, scrubbed

Place potatoes on a baking sheet. Bake for 1 hour at 425° or until soft when pricked with a knife. Remove from oven and cut in half lengthwise. Scoop out the pulp, being careful to leave the shell intact.

Place pulp into mixing bowl.

1/3 cup butter
2 tsp. salt
1/8 tsp. pepper
1/2 cup milk
1/2 cup sour cream

Add these next 5 ingredients to the pulp and whip until light and fluffy.

Refill shells with the mashed potatoes. Return to baking sheet.

1/2 - 1 cup shredded cheddar
    cheese

Bake at 325° for 20 minutes. Top with the shredded cheese for the last 5 minutes.

The stuffed shells may be refrigerated overnight before baking.

-Ruth

Hashbrown Casserole

26 oz. frozen country style
hashbrowns

1/2 cup melted butter
1 tsp. salt
1/4 tsp. pepper
dash of garlic powder
1/3 cup chopped onions
1 (10 3/4 oz.) can cream of
mushroom soup*
1 1/2 cups sour cream*
2 cups shredded cheddar cheese

*The light or fat free variety of
these two items works well in
this recipe.

*Remove hashbrowns from freezer
about 1/2 hour before your
preparation time.*
*Pour hashbrowns into a large
mixing bowl and add remaining
ingredients, stir until the seasonings
and cheese are thoroughly mixed.*

*Place into a greased 9"x13" baking
dish. Bake uncovered at 350° for
50 - 60 minutes, stirring once or
twice during baking time.
Remove from oven and let set about
5 minutes before serving.*

Serves 8 - 10.

I often serve these potatoes with meatloaf (see recipe on
page 103) and garlic green beans (page 120).

Laughter is
brightest where
food is best.
- Irish Proverb

-Carolyn

Creamy Scalloped Potatoes

5 lbs. potatoes, peeled & cut

Place the potatoes in a large saucepan and cover with water, cook until tender, but not soft. Drain and cool. Shred the cooled potatoes.

1/2 cup butter, melted
16 oz. sour cream
2 (10 3/4 oz.) cans cream of
    celery soup
1/2 lb. Velveeta cheese, cubed
milk

Combine the butter, sour cream, soup and cheese, gently stir into the shredded potatoes and add enough milk to make a creamy mixture.

Optional additions:
1 lb. fried hamburger
    or
1 lb. ham, cooked and cubed

Place into a baking dish, cover and bake at 325° for 1 hour, or until heated through.

This can also be prepared and refrigerated overnight.

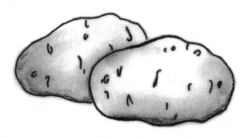

Credit for this recipe goes to Hannah Stoltzfus. One summer when we both were counselors at a youth camp, she prepared this dish ahead of time, baked it at camp, and it was delicious! I've used the recipe a lot ever since. Hannah and her husband Amos now run a very successful catering business.

-Ruth

Sweet Sweet Potatoes

2 - 3 medium sweet potatoes -
    peeled and sliced
3 Tbsp. butter

salt
pepper
2 Tbsp. brown sugar, heaping

Melt the butter in a large skillet.
Add the sliced sweet potatoes.

Turn heat to medium-low and
simmer, covered, for 10 - 15
minutes or until tender, stirring
occasionally.

Add the salt and pepper (to taste)
and the brown sugar. Stir gently
and simmer for another minute.

Remove from heat and serve.
May be served with a sprinkle of
parsley for nice color.

*For a decorative look,
slice the potatoes with a
crinkle style slicer.

This is a 'sweetly' remembered dish from Mom that my
family enjoys as a side dish.

-Ruth

Mushroom and Garlic Green Beans

Although this recipe is written to be used with canned green beans, it's even better with the fresh-from-the-garden ones as well. Just cook in water until tender before adding to the melted butter in skillet.

3 Tbsp. butter

1 tsp. garlic powder, or two
    garlic cloves, minced
1/4 tsp. salt
dash of pepper
1/2 cup sliced fresh mushrooms

1 quart green beans

Melt the butter in a medium sized skillet on medium heat, add the garlic, mushrooms and seasonings. Sauté for approximately 3 - 5 minutes.

Reduce to low heat, add the beans and stir gently. Continue to heat for another 8 - 10 minutes, stirring frequently.

Serves 4.

This is an easy way to dress up green beans. Other additions that may be more pleasing to your taste buds could be:

2 Tbsp. chopped onions, in
    place of the garlic.

1 - 2 slices bacon, cut into 1 in.
    pieces and lightly
    browned in skillet
    before adding beans, in
    place of the butter.

-Carolyn

Cheesy Green Beans

2 1/2 lbs. French cut frozen
    green beans
1 cup water
1 1/2 tsp. salt

1/2 cup butter
1 cup Velveeta cheese
2 tsp. Accent
1 tsp. pepper

Place green beans in medium-sized
saucepan; add the water and salt;
bring to a gentle boil and cook until
the beans are crisp-tender.

Add the remaining ingredients and
stir gently till the cheese is melted.

Serves 20.

I like to make this vegetable for special meals because my
three sons-in-law enjoy green beans, while some of them
don't enjoy a lot of the other vegetables.
-Mom

 # Creamed
Vegetable Casserole

1 Tbsp. butter
1 Tbsp. flour
dash pepper
1 cup milk

3 cups steamed vegetables,
    drained
2 cups herb seasoned stuffing

1 cup herb seasoned stuffing
2 Tbsp. butter, melted

1 cup shredded cheddar cheese

Melt the butter in a small
saucepan; stir in the flour and
pepper, until smooth. Add the milk
and cook over medium heat until
thick and bubbly. Cook and stir
another 1 - 2 minutes. Stir in the
vegetables and 2 cups bread crumbs,
then pour into a 1 qt. baking dish.

Mix the remaining cup of bread
crumbs with the butter and sprinkle
over the top of the casserole. Bake
uncovered at 350° for 20 - 25
minutes.

-Hannah

Squash Casserole

2 cups yellow summer squash,
    cubed

Place into small saucepan; cover with water and cook until tender. Drain and set aside.

2 eggs
1 cup milk
1/4 cup butter, melted
1/2 tsp. salt
pinch of pepper

Beat the eggs. Add the milk, butter, salt and pepper and beat again.

1 cup cracker crumbs

Stir the cracker crumbs into the egg mixture and let stand for several minutes.

1 cup Velveeta cheese, cubed
1/4 cup chopped onions

Add the squash, cheese and onions to the egg mixture and stir until ingredients are well blended. Spoon into a 2 quart baking dish. Bake at 350° for 30 - 35 minutes.

You may cover the top of casserole with cheese slices 5 minutes before finished baking.

Serves 5 - 6.

-Hannah

Zucchini Squash Casserole

4 - 6 small zucchini (6 - 8 cups), cubed
1 tsp. salt

Place the zucchini and salt into a medium-sized sauce pan, cook until tender. Drain and set aside.

2 Tbsp. butter
1/2 cup chopped onion
1 cup coarsely shredded carrots, optional

Sauté the onions and carrots in the butter until tender.

1 (10 3/4 oz.) can cream of mushroom soup
1/2 cup sour cream

Add the soup and sour cream to the sautéed vegetables and mix well.

3 cups herb seasoned croutons

1/2 cup shredded cheddar cheese

Gently stir the zucchini and bread crumbs into the above mixture. Place into a 9"x13" baking dish and top with the shredded cheese.

Bake uncovered at 350° for 30 - 40 minutes or until heated through and bubbly.

-Karla

Calico Beans

The following recipe is from a family friend, Jean Mast, whose friendship (and this recipe) dates back to the time our family and theirs lived in South Carolina. Jean now resides in Antrim, Ohio, next door to Carolyn who reports that Jean is the perfect 'can-I-borrow-a-cup-of-flour' and 'here's-a-fresh-loaf-of-bread-for-you' neighbor. It's a small world after all!

1/4 lb. bacon
1 lb. hamburger
1/2 cup chopped onion

Brown the bacon and hamburger with the onions in a large skillet. Place into a medium-sized mixing bowl.

1/2 cup brown sugar
1/2 cup ketchup
2 Tbsp. vinegar
1 Tbsp. prepared mustard
1 tsp. salt
1 (17 oz.) can lima beans
1 (15.5 oz.) can kidney beans
1 (28 oz.) can pork n' beans

Add the remaining ingredients and mix well. Pour into a 2 1/2 qt. baking dish and bake at 200° for 1 1/2 hours.

-Ruth

Summer Bean Casserole

12 oz. bacon

Fry bacon until crisp. Set aside 2 Tbsp. of the drippings. (Oscar Meyer's center cut is my favorite bacon.) Set aside.

1/2 lb. ground beef
1 Tbsp. bacon drippings

Brown the beef in the bacon drippings. Set aside.

1/2 cup chopped onions
1/2 cup chopped bell peppers
1 Tbsp. bacon drippings

Sauté the onions and peppers in the drippings. Set aside.

2 (15 oz.) cans pork n' beans
1 (16 oz.) can Bush's mixed
   beans
1 (14 1/2 oz.) can lima beans

Combine the bacon, beef and vegetables in a 3-quart baking dish. Add the beans.

1/3 cup barbecue sauce
1/3 cup ketchup
1/4 cup brown sugar
1/4 cup honey
1 Tbsp. Dijon mustard
1 tsp. salt
1 tsp. pepper
1/2 tsp. cayenne pepper

Combine the remaining ingredients in a medium mixing bowl and add to the bean mixture.
Stir and and bake at 350° for 1 hour.

No matter where I take my guests... it seems they like my kitchen best.
-Pa. Dutch saying

-Marti

Pasta Primavera

2 lb. asparagus

Remove the tough ends and scales from the asparagus. Cut diagonally into 1 1/2 pieces. Steam over boiling water about 6 - 8 minutes or until crisp-tender. Remove from heat and set aside.

1 medium onion, chopped
1 clove garlic, minced
1 Tbsp. cooking oil

Sauté the onion and garlic in a large skillet until tender.

1 large carrot, sliced
1 medium sweet red pepper, chopped
1/2 cup fresh or canned mushrooms, sliced

Add the carrots, peppers and mushrooms to the onion mixture. Sauté until crisp-tender. Remove from heat and drain.

1 cup whipping cream
1/2 cup chicken broth
2 tsp. basil
1/2 tsp. salt
1/4 tsp. pepper

Combine all these ingredients in a medium saucepan. Cook over medium heat for 5 minutes, stirring occasionally.

8 oz. linguine or spaghetti noodles, broken

Cook according to package directions. Drain and place into a large serving bowl. Add the vegetables and cream mixture and toss gently.

1 cup parmesan cheese

Sprinkle the cheese over the top and serve immediately.

Makes 8 servings.

-Marti

Rice Pilaf

This recipe is for a large crowd and goes well with fried chicken breasts and peas and carrots. If you are preparing individual plates, a sprig of parsley and a slice of tomato on a each plate gives a picture perfect look!

8 cups (uncooked) long grain rice
4 cups celery, chopped
2 cups onions, chopped
1 cup butter, melted
16 cups liquid (I use a mixture of water and chicken broth
4 tsp. Worcestershire sauce
4 tsp. soy sauce
4 tsp. thyme
4 tsp. oregano

Mix all these ingredients together and divide into 2 12 quart roasting pans.

Cover and bake at 325° for 1 hour.

Serves 50.

-Mom

Fried Rice

or Vegetable and/or Shrimp Fried Rice

2 Tbsp. butter
1 1/2 cup uncooked rice

Melt butter in a large frying pan, add the rice and sauté for 5 minutes on medium heat. Set aside.

2 1/2 cups water or chicken broth
2 Tbsp. soy sauce
1/4 cup butter
1 cup frozen mixed vegetables (corn, peas, carrots), optional
1 cup small shrimp, optional

1 - 2 eggs

Combine these 3 ingredients in a medium saucepan and bring to a boil. You may add one or both of the optional ingredients if desired Add fried rice. Simmer over low heat for approximately 20 minutes or until rice is dry.
Scramble eggs in same frying pan; chop into small pieces and add to cooked rice.

-Marti

Not what we have, but what we enjoy constitutes our abundance.

-Anonymous

Pies

PIES

Flaky Pie Crust

4 cups flour
1 Tbsp. sugar
2 tsp. salt
1 3/4 cup shortening, butter
    flavor

1/2 cup water
1 Tbsp. vinegar
1 egg

Combine dry ingredients.

Cut in shortening and mix until it becomes crumbly.

Mix the last three ingredients together, then add to the flour mixture. Mixing just until well blended.

Makes 5 pie crusts.

-Mom & Ruth

Easy, Flaky Pie Crusts

4 cups flour
1 tsp. baking powder
1 1/2 tsp. salt
1 1/2 cup shortening, butter
    flavor

1 egg, beaten
1 Tbsp. vinegar
1/2 cup cold water

Combine the flour, baking powder and salt. I use my mixer with dough or regular hook.
Add the shortening and mix until it resembles coarse crumbs.
Add the remaining ingredients, mixing just until well moistened. Remove from mixing bowl and divide into 4 equal parts, Roll out and press into pie pans. Unfilled shells should be baked at 375° for 15 minutes.

-Carolyn

Lemon Cream Pie

1/2 cup water 4 Tbsp. cornstarch	*Combine the cornstarch and water, stirring until smooth; set aside.*
1 1/2 cups water 1 cup sugar	*Combine the water and sugar in a double boiler and heat to boiling. Add the cornstarch mixture and cook until it begins to thicken.*
3 egg yolks, slightly beaten	*Add the egg yolks; cook for 3 - 5 minutes. Remove from heat.*
1 Tbsp. butter 1/4 tsp. salt the juice and grated rind of 1 lemon	*Add the butter, salt, lemon rind and juice and blend well.*
1 - 9" baked pie shell whipped topping	*Let cool and pour into the pie shell. Top with the whipped topping and serve.*

-Ruth

Cherry Pie

1 - 9" unbaked pie crust

1 cup water
2 Tbsp. clear jel or cornstarch
3/4 cup sugar

3 cups cherries
2 Tbsp. cherry gelatin
1/2 tsp. almond extract

Topping:
3/4 cup flour
1/2 cup brown sugar
1/4 cup butter, softened

Combine the water and sugar in a medium saucepan. Add cornstarch while stirring with wire whisk. Bring to a boil and cook until thickened.

Add gelatin and almond extract and stir. Stir in cherries; pour into unbaked pie crust.

Combine flour and sugar; add butter and mix until crumbs form. Sprinkle over pie.
Bake at 375° for 30 - 40 minutes.

-Ruth

Frozen Peanut Butter Pie

1 pkg. (3 oz.) cream cheese, softened
1 cup confectioners sugar
1/2 cup crunchy *or* creamy peanut butter
1/2 cup milk

3 cups whipped topping

1 - 9" baked or graham cracker pie shell

whipped topping
chopped peanuts

Whip the cream cheese until light and fluffy.
Beat in the sugar and peanut butter.

Add the milk slowly, blending thoroughly. Fold in the whipped topping.
Pour into the pie shell. Freeze. When ready to serve, garnish with whipped topping and sprinkle chopped peanuts on top. Serve.

-Hannah

Frozen Pina Colada Pie

3 oz. cream cheese, softened
1 Tbsp. sugar
1/2 cup milk
1 (8 oz.) can crushed pineapple,
 drained
1 1/3 cup angel flake
 coconut

8 oz. whipped topping, thawed
1 - 9" graham cracker crust

Combine the cream cheese, sugar,
milk, coconut and 1/2 cup of the
pineapple in a blender. Mix well.

Fold the whipped topping into the
cream cheese mixture. Spoon into
the crust. Freeze until firm, about 4
hours.
Let stand at room temperature for 5
minutes.
Garnish with remaining pineapple;
cut and serve.

-Hannah

Key Lime Pie

8 oz. cream cheese, softened
1 (14 oz.) can sweetened
 condensed milk

1/2 cup key lime juice

8 oz. sour crm.
8 oz. whipped topping
green food coloring, optional

whipped topping
lime slices

Place the cream cheese and milk
into a mixing bowl and mix until
smooth and creamy.

Add the lime juice, mixing well.

Fold in the whipped topping and
add a drop of green food coloring for
a slight green tint to pie if desired.
Pour into baked pie shell.
Top with whipped topping and lime
slices.

This makes a cool and refreshing summer dessert!

-Mom

Peach Pie

5 peaches, peeled and thinly
    sliced*
1/2 cup sugar

water

1 (3 oz.) box lemon gelatin
2 cups vanilla ice cream

1 - 9" baked or graham cracker
    pie crust
whipped topping

*An egg slicer does a beautiful
job slicing peach halves.

Stir sugar into the peaches; set in refrigerator for 20 minutes. Remove and drain the juice from the peaches into a one-cup measure. Return the peaches to the refrigerator.

Add water to the drained juice to equal one cup. Pour into a 2 quart saucepan and heat to boiling. Remove from heat; add lemon gelatin to heated juice, stirring till dissolved. Add ice cream; stir until mixture is creamy. Refrigerate until partially set. Remove and gently fold in the peach slices.

Pour into the pie shell and refrigerate for 2 - 3 hours or until set. Top with whipped topping before serving.

This recipe is from a friend and great cook, Doris (Miller) Vetter who lived with us for about a year. Her positive attitude toward life always inspired me. She is now married with two children and resides in her hometown in Indiana.

-Ruth

Apple Crumb Pie

1 cup sugar
3/4 cup water

2 Tbsp. clear jel
1/4 cup water
1 Tbsp. butter
1/2 tsp. cinnamon

3 cups diced Granny Smith
    apples (3 - 4 apples)
1 - 9" unbaked pie shell

Crumb topping;
3/4 cup flour
1/2 cup brown sugar
1/4 cup butter, softened

Combine sugar and water in a medium saucepan; bring to a boil.

*Combine the clear jel and water and add to boiling mixture while stirring with wire whisk.
Add cinnamon and butter and continue cooking until thickened.*

Add apples; stir till well coated. Remove from heat; pour into unbaked pie shell.

Combine topping ingredients; mix until crumbly. Sprinkle over pie and bake at 375° for 30 - 40 minutes.

-Ruth

Double Crust Apple Pie

2 cups water
3/4 cup brown sugar
1/2 cup white sugar
3 1/2 Tbsp. clear jell

2 1/2 cups peeled and diced
    apples

1 tsp. cinnamon
1/4 tsp. salt

2 - 9" pie dough rounds, one
    pressed into a 9" pie pan,
    one reserved for top crust.

*Place the first 4 ingredients into a medium saucepan and stir until sugar and clear jel is dissolved, heat to boiling. Stir with whisk continuously until the mixture is transparent and thickened.
Pour over the apples and seasonings and gently stir.*

Pour into an unbaked pie shell and cover with second pie shell. Cut slits or designs into top shell, for vents, crimp edges. Brush top with evaporated milk and sprinkle with cinnamon and sugar. Bake at 350° until golden brown, 45 - 50 minutes.

-Mom

Fresh Strawberry Pie

1 cup white sugar
1 1/2 cups water
1/4 cup strawberry gelatin
2 Tbsp. light corn syrup

Place the first four ingredients in a 3-quart saucepan and heat until gelatin and sugar are dissolved.

1/4 cup clear jel
1/4 cup water

Dissolve the clear jel in water; gradually add to the hot mixture and continue stirring and cooking until thickened and clear. Cool until partially set.

1 quart strawberries, cleaned
　　and sliced
1- 9" baked pie shell

whipped topping

Fold in sliced berries. Pour into the pie shell.
Chill for several hours.

Top with the whipped topping and serve.

-Kathleen

Strawberry Fans:
Using a firm, ripe strawberry, place green top down on a cutting surface; make cuts into berry, being careful not to slice all the way through. Gently fan out the slices.
Strawberry fans are nice as a garnish for pies, cakes, salads, etc.

Strawberry
Cream Cheese Pie

This delicious recipe came from a friend, Mary Lois Yoder, who won a blue ribbon for it. It takes a little more time and planning ahead than most pie recipes, but it is well worth the time if you enjoy cheesecake!

1 cup graham cracker crumbs
6 Tbsp. butter, softened
3 Tbsp. brown sugar
1 tsp. cinnamon

Preheat oven to 300°. Blend these four ingredients with a fork, until well blended. Press into the bottom and sides of a 9" deep dish pie pan. (I like the pottery ones.) Set aside.

12 oz. cream cheese, softened
2 eggs
1/2 cup sugar
1 Tbsp. vanilla

Blend together the cream cheese, eggs, vanilla and sugar just until well blended.
Pour into crust and bake for 30 - 35 minutes or until set; remove from oven and let cool for 20-30 minutes.

1 cup sour cream
1 tsp. vanilla
3 tsp. white sugar

Combine the next three ingredients and spread over the cheesecake. Bake an additional 15 minutes. Chill.

2 Tbsp. clear jel or cornstarch
1 1/2 Tbsp. strawberry gelatin
1/2 cup water
1/2 cup white sugar

Place the next 4 ingredients into a medium-sized saucepan and mix with a wire whisk. Place over medium heat and bring to a boil, stirring constantly, until thickened. Allow this to come to room temperature.

1 1/2 cup sliced strawberries*

*Any fresh fruit that you enjoy can be substituted here, just be sure to choose a gelatin flavor that complements that fruit.

Layer the strawberry slices over the chilled pie (Mary Lois arranges them in a circular, flower-like pattern) and spread the cooled glaze over the berries. Top with whipped topping if desired.

-Carolyn

Pecan Pie

1 unbaked 9" pie shell
1 cup pecan halves or pieces

If pie shell is frozen, let thaw. Place pecans evenly in bottom of pie pan.

3 eggs
2/3 cup sugar
1/2 tsp. salt
1/3 cup butter, melted
1 cup light corn syrup

Combine all ingredients in a blender or food processor and mix just until well blended. Pour over the pecans. Bake at 350° for 40 - 45 minutes. Center will be slightly shaky when done.

This easy but delicious recipe come from my mother-in-law, Edna Miller. Not only does she serve up wonderful meals when we go to her house, but she also has that special Mother-hospitality that makes us
-Carolyn

German Chocolate Pie

1 pkg. (4 oz.) German chocolate
2 Tbsp. milk

Place into large microwaveable bowl and microwave on medium heat until melted, stirring occasionally.

3 oz. cream cheese, softened
2 Tbsp. sugar
1/4 cup milk

Add the next 3 ingredients to the melted chocolate and beat with electric mixture until well blended. Refrigerate about 10 minutes.

8 oz. whipped topping, thawed

Fold the whipped topping into the chilled mixture, stirring until well blended and smooth.

1 - 9" graham cracker crust

Pour into the crust. Freeze until firm, about 4 hours. Garnish with chocolate curls or shavings if desired.

-Marti

139

Silk Chocolate Pie

1 pkg. (4 oz.) Bakers German
   sweet chocolate
2 Tbsp. milk

Microwave the chocolate along with
the milk on high at 20 - 30 second
intervals until chocolate is melted,
stirring frequently.

6 oz. cream cheese, softened
1/4 cup milk
3 Tbsp. sugar

Beat the cream cheese, sugar and
milk until smooth; add the
chocolate and mix until well
blended. Refrigerate for 10
minutes.

4 cups whipped topping

2 baked or graham cracker pie
   crusts

Fold in the whipped topping and
spoon into the prepared crusts. May
freeze if desired, or use within a
day.

Top with whipped topping and
chocolate curls for garnish.

-Mom

Cinnamon Custard Pie

2 cups milk
2 Tbsp. butter

Place milk and butter into medium
saucepan and heat till butter melts.
Set aside.

3 eggs
1/4 tsp. salt
3/4 cup sugar
1 tsp. vanilla
1 1/2 tsp. cinnamon

1 - 9" pie crust

Separate one of the eggs and whip
the white of that egg. Set aside. Mix
the eggs and remaining egg yolk
with the next 4 ingredients, then
add the heated milk. Fold in the
whipped egg white.

Pour into the unbaked pie shell and
bake at 325° for 35 - 40 minutes or
until center is set.

-Ruth

Bob Andy Pie
(Mom's Cinnamon Custard Pie)

I'm not sure how this pie came by its name. In my growing up years it was considered an 'everyday' pie, not one you would have for Sunday dinners. Now it's a special treat that I make when Carolyn comes home to visit. It's one of her favorites and she thinks it tastes even better when called by its old-fashioned name!

3 eggs, separated

After separating the eggs, beat the whites in a cold metal dish with clean beaters, until stiff. Then beat the yolks. Set aside.

2 cups white sugar
4 Tbsp. flour
2 tsp. cinnamon
1 1/2 Tbsp. butter, melted

4 cups evaporated milk

2 - 9" unbaked pie crusts

Combine the dry ingredients. Add the butter, beaten egg yolks and milk, adding the milk last and gradually, mixing well after each addition.
Fold in the beaten egg whites, then pour the mixture into the pie crusts. Bake at 350° for 40 - 45 minutes, or until center is firm.

Makes 2 pies.

-Mom

Chocolate Cream Pie

2 squares chocolate *or*
   3 Tbsp. cocoa

Melt chocolate in top of double boiler.

1 1/2 cups milk

Add the milk and bring to boiling point.

1/2 cup milk
3/4 cup sugar
1/2 tsp. salt
3 Tbsp. cornstarch

Combine the sugar, salt and cornstarch with the 1/2 cup milk to form a smooth paste. Add the paste to the heated milk and chocolate; cook until thickened.

2 egg yolks

Beat the egg yolks, and pour a small amount of the hot mixture over the yolks before adding them to the pudding mixture; cook an additional 2 minutes.

1 Tbsp. butter
1 tsp. vanilla

Remove from the heat and add the butter and vanilla.

1 - 9" baked pie shell
whipped topping

Cool and pour into the pie shell. Chill and top with meringue or whipped topping prior to serving.

-Ruth

Coconut Cream Pie

1 1/2 cups milk

Scald milk in the top of a double boiler.

4 Tbsp. corn starch
1/2 tsp. salt
1/2 cup sugar
1/2 cup milk

Combine the corn starch, salt, and sugar with the milk until it forms a smooth paste. Pour into the scalded milk and cook until thickened, stirring frequently with a wire whip.

2 egg yolks

Beat the egg yolks and mix a small amount of the pudding mixture with the yolks, then add to the hot mixture. Cook and stir an additional 2 minutes.

1 Tbsp. butter
1 tsp. vanilla
3/4 cup shredded coconut

Remove from the heat and add the butter, vanilla and coconut, stirring until well blended. Cool.

1 - 9" baked pie shell

whipped topping
1/2 cup coconut, toasted

Pour into the pie shell and top with the whipped topping. Sprinkle the toasted coconut over the topping and chill until ready to serve.

A crust eaten in peace is better than a banquet partaken in anxiety.
-Aesop

-Ruth

Vanilla Crumb Pie

Bottom layer;
1/2 cup brown sugar
1/2 cup dark molasses
1 Tbsp. flour
1 egg, beaten
1/2 cup water
1/2 cup milk
1 tsp. vanilla

Place all ingredients for bottom layer in a 4 quart saucepan. Cook over medium heat; stirring with wire whisk until thickened.
Pour into unbaked pie shell.

Top layer:
1 cup flour
1/2 cup brown sugar
1/2 tsp. baking soda
1/2 tsp. baking powder
1/4 cup butter flavored
  shortening

Combine the dry ingredients; add the shortening and mix until crumbly.
Gently place crumb mixture over bottom layer in pie shell.
Bake at 375° for 40 - 45 minutes.

1 - 9" unbaked pie shell

-Ruth

Basic Cream Pie

1 - 9" baked pie crust

Have ready.

1 3/4 cups milk

Heat milk in double boiler to boiling .

1/2 cup sugar
1/4 tsp. salt
2 Tbsp. cornstarch
3 Tbsp. flour
1/2 cup milk

Combine the sugar, salt, cornstarch and flour in a small bowl. Add the 1/2 cup milk and stir until it forms a smooth paste. Stir the paste into the hot milk. Cook, stirring constantly until thickened. Cover and cook another 4 - 5 minutes, stirring occasionally.

3 egg yolks

Lightly beat the egg yolks and add a small amount of the hot custard to the yolks, then stir into the mixture. Cook an additional 2 minutes, stirring constantly. Remove from heat.

1 Tbsp. butter
1 tsp. vanilla

whipped topping

Add the butter and vanilla, stirring until well blended.
Cool slightly and pour into the baked crust. (see variations below)
Top with whipped topping.

Butterscotch cream pie: Use 3/4 cup brown sugar in place of the 1/2 cup white sugar.
Chocolate cream pie: Add a 1 oz. square of unsweetened chocolate to the cold milk. Add an additional 1/4 cup sugar. Sprinkle chocolate curls over the whipped topping.
Coconut cream pie: Add 2/3 cup angel flake coconut and 1/2 tsp. coconut flavoring (opt.) to the custard after removing from heat. Toast 1/3 cup of flaked coconut and sprinkle over the whipped topping.
Peanut butter cream pie: (our favorite) Mix together 3/4 cup powdered sugar and 1/2 cup peanut butter until crumbly. Sprinkle 2/3 of the crumbs in pie shell before pouring in the custard. Sprinkle the remaining crumbs over the whipped topping.

-Carolyn

Creative ways to finish a pie crust...

...and a good way to use your pie dough scraps.

Roll out the scraps to the same thickness as your crusts and cut out shapes using a knife or cookie cutter. An apple on an apple pie, leaf or pumpkin on pumpkin pie, etc. Use a knife to lightly score markings for a realistic look.

If you do leaves, arrange them around the edge of your finished pie crust and/or the center of the pie....or place a leaf on each slice.

These can be baked with the pie or baked separately on a cookie sheet; then placed on the finished pie.

Cakes
and
Desserts

CAKES AND DESSERTS

Chocolate Fudge Cake

4 (1 oz.) unsweetened chocolate
squares

*Place chocolate in top of a double
boiler or microwave safe bowl and
melt. Set aside, cool.*

1 (8 oz.) pkg. cream cheese,
softened
1 egg
1/4 cup sugar
3 Tbsp. milk
2 Tbsp. butter, softened
1 Tbsp. cornstarch
1/2 tsp. vanilla

*Combine the cream cheese, egg, and
sugar in medium mixing bowl; beat
until smooth and creamy.
Gradually add the milk, while
continuing to beat. Then add the
butter, cornstarch and vanilla.
Mixing well. Set aside.*

1/2 cup butter, softened
2 cups sugar
2 eggs

*Cream the butter; add the sugar and
mix well. Add the eggs and blend in
well.*

2 cups all purpose flour
1 tsp. baking powder
1/2 tsp. baking soda
1/4 tsp. salt
1 1/3 cups milk

1 tsp. vanilla

*Combine the 4 dry ingredients. Add
to the creamed mixture alternately
with the milk. Mix well after each
addition.
Stir in the melted chocolate and the
vanilla.
Pour 1/2 of the chocolate batter into
a greased and floured 13"x9" baking
pan. Spoon the reserved cream cheese
mixture evenly over the chocolate
batter. Then top with the remaining
1/2 of chocolate batter. Bake 350°
for
55 - 60 minutes or until wooden pick
inserted in center comes out clean.
Cool completely.*

Ice with Fudge icing.

Fudge icing:

1 (1 oz.) squares unsweetened
chocolate
1/4 cup butter
3 1/2 cups powdered sugar,
sifted
1/3 cup milk
1 tsp. vanilla

*Place the chocolate and butter in top
of double boiler and melt. Remove
from the heat and let cool.
Add the powdered sugar and milk to
the melted chocolate and beat at
medium speed until smooth. Stir in
vanilla.*

-Marti

Easy Chocolate Cake

This is a moist and simple recipe and is a good way to get your youngsters started with baking duties!

2 cups sugar
3 cups flour
3 Tbsp. cocoa, heaping
2 tsp. soda
1/2 tsp. salt
3/4 cup cooking oil
2 Tbsp. vinegar
1 Tbsp. vanilla
2 cups cold water

Place all ingredients into a large mixing bowl and mix thoroughly.

Pour batter into a 9"x13" pan and bake at 350° for 45 minutes.

This can also be used for making cupcakes. Bake at 350° for 20 minutes.

-Hannah

Poppy Seed Cake

1 cup vegetable oil
3 eggs
2 1/4 cups sugar

3 cups all-purpose flour
1 1/2 tsp. baking powder
1 1/2 tsp. salt
1 1/2 cups milk

1 1/2 tsp. almond extract
1 1/2 tsp. butter flavoring
1/3 cup poppy seeds

Combine the oil, eggs and sugar in a large mixing bowl; beat at medium speed for 2 minutes.

Combine the flour, baking powder, and salt; add to the egg mixture alternately with the milk. Mix well after each addition.

Stir in the flavorings and poppy seeds.

Pour the batter into a greased and floured 10" tube pan. Bake at 350° for 45 - 55 minutes or until a wooden pick inserted in center comes out clean.
Cool in pan 10 minutes; remove from pan, and place on a serving plate. While still warm, prick cake at 1" intervals with a wooden pick. Pour the glaze (recipe follows) over the cake.

Glaze:
1/2 cup sugar
1/4 cup orange juice
1/2 tsp. almond extract
1/2 tsp. butter flavoring
1/2 tsp. vanilla extract

Combine all ingredients in a small mixing bowl; beat at medium speed of an electric mixer until well blended. The mixture will be slightly grainy.

-Ruth

Hummingbird Cake

3 cups flour
2 cups sugar
1 tsp. salt
1 tsp. baking soda
1 tsp. cinnamon

Combine the dry ingredients and stir with a large spoon.

1 1/2 tsp. vanilla
1 1/2 cups oil
3 eggs

Combine the oil, vanilla and eggs and beat with electric mixer till light. Add to the dry mixture; stir with spoon.

1 1/2 cups pineapple, crushed
   and undrained
1 1/2 cups bananas, mashed
1/2 cup nuts, chopped

Fold in pineapple, bananas and nuts.

Divide the batter between three 9" greased and floured pans. Bake at 300° for 30 minutes or until pick inserted in center comes out clean. Cool.

Cream Cheese Icing:
1/2 cup butter, softened
1 (8 oz.) pkg. cream cheese,
   softened

Cream the butter and cream cheese until smooth and creamy.

3 - 4 cups powdered sugar
1 tsp. vanilla
1 - 2 Tbsp. milk

Add the sugar, vanilla and milk and mix till it comes to spreadable consistency.

Layer the cakes and icing and finish by icing the sides and top of the three layers.

This is a very good seller at my Bake Shop.
The icing makes the cake!

-Mom

Texas Sheet Cake

1 cup butter
1 cup water
4 Tbsp. cocoa

Melt the butter in a medium saucepan and add the water and cocoa; bring to a boil.

2 cups sugar
2 cups flour
1/2 tsp. salt
1 tsp. soda
2 eggs
1 tsp. vanilla
1/2 cup sour cream

Place the remaining ingredients in a large mixing bowl; add above mixture. Beat together.
Pour batter into an 11"x16" sheet cake pan and bake at 350° for 30 minutes.
Frost with following recipe while still warm.

Frosting:
1/2 cup butter
3 Tbsp. cocoa
1/3 cup milk
3 - 4 cups powdered sugar
1 cup pecans, optional
1 tsp. vanilla

Melt butter in small saucepan, add cocoa and milk. Bring to a boil and add the nuts and vanilla. Beat and add sugar till spreading consistency.

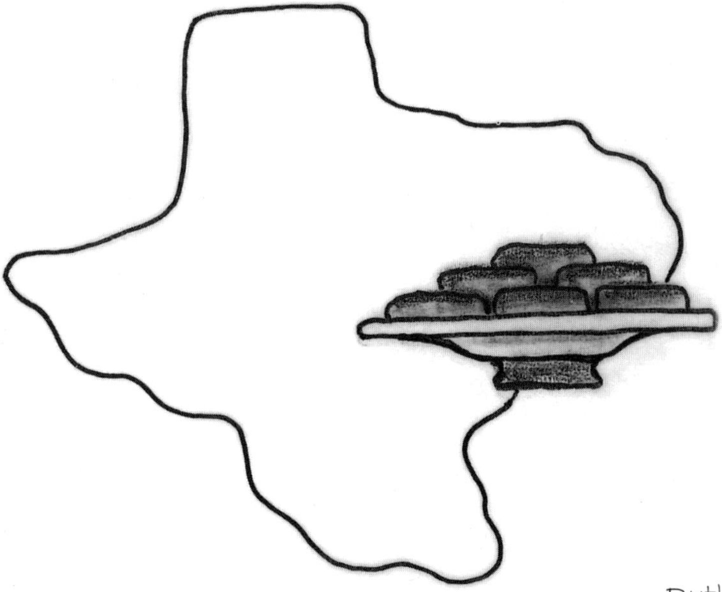

-Ruth

Ho-Ho Cake

1 yellow cake mix

Prepare and bake cake according to package directions. Pour batter into into a greased jellyroll pan. Bake and cool.

1 1/4 cups milk
5 Tbsp. flour

Combine the milk and flour in a medium saucepan and cook while stirring with a wire whisk until thickened. Cool completely.

1/2 cup butter
1 cup sugar
1/2 cup shortening

Add the butter, sugar and shortening; beat until smooth and creamy. Spread over cooled cake. Set cake in refrigerator while mixing icing.

Icing:
3 cups powdered sugar
1/3 cup cocoa
1 Tbsp. vanilla
1/2 cup butter, softened
1/8 - 1/4 cup evaporated milk

Combine all the icing ingredients, using only 1/8 cup of the evaporated milk, beat till creamy and add more milk as needed for a nice spreadable consistency. You may add more powdered sugar if you get it too runny. Spread over cream layer on cake and serve.

I'm not sure where this cake came by its name, but it's rich chocolatey icing is a delight to the taste buds! It was first introduced to me by my sister-in-law, Shelby. Shelby is one of those hostesses whose house emits that relaxed 'come in and make yourself at home' feeling!

-Carolyn

Oatmeal Cake

1 1/4 cup boiling water
1 cup quick oats

Pour the boiling water over the oatmeal and set aside.

1/2 cup butter, softened
1 cup brown sugar
1 cup sugar
2 eggs

Cream butter and sugars; add eggs, beating well after each one.

1 1/2 cup flour
1 tsp. cinnamon
1 tsp. baking soda
1/2 tsp. salt
1 tsp. vanilla

Sift the dry ingredients together; add to the creamed mixture alternating with the oatmeal mixture. Add vanilla and beat till well blended.

Pour batter into a greased and floured 9"x13" baking pan.
Bake at 350° for 30 - 35 minutes.
Remove from oven and while still hot, top with the following mixture.

Topping:
2/3 cup brown sugar
1 cup chopped nuts
1 cup angel flake coconut
6 Tbsp. butter, melted
1/4 cup evaporated milk
1 tsp. vanilla
pinch of salt

Blend all topping ingredients together and spread evenly over hot cake.
Place under broiler for 2 - 3 minutes or until topping is browned.

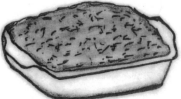

-Carolyn

Cream Cheese Pound Cake

1 cup butter, softened
1 (8 oz.) pkg. cream cheese,
   softened
3 cups sugar

*Cream butter and cream cheese;
gradually add the sugar, beating on
medium mixer speed till light and
fluffy.*

6 eggs

*Add the eggs, one at a time, beating
well after each addition.*

3 cups cake flour, sifted
1 tsp. vanilla extract

*Add the flour, mixing just until well
blended. Stir in vanilla.*

*Pour batter into a greased and
floured 10" tube pan. Bake at 325°
for 1 hour and 15 minutes or until
a wooden pick inserted in center
comes out clean.
Let cake cool in pan for 10
minutes. Remove and cool.*

-Ruth

Million Dollar Pound Cake

1 lb. butter, softened
3 cups sugar

Cream butter and sugar till light and fluffy.

6 eggs

Add eggs, mixing well after each addition.

4 cups cake flour
3/4 cup milk
1 tsp. vanilla extract
1 tsp. almond extract, optional

Add flour alternately with milk and flavorings, mixing just until well blended.

Pour batter into a greased 10" tube pan and bake at 300° for 1 hour and 20 minutes.

This cake has a light and buttery flavor. It's a good cake for a neighborhood ice cream social, served with ice cream and fresh strawberries.

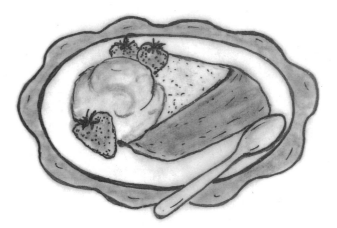

-Mom

Yellow Layer Cake

2 cups flour
1 1/3 cup sugar
1/2 cup butter flavored
    shortening
2/3 cup milk

Combine the first 4 ingredients in a large mixing bowl; mix.

3 tsp. baking powder
1 tsp. salt
1 tsp. vanilla
2 eggs
1/3 cup milk

Add the remaining ingredients and mix until well blended, continue mixing on medium speed for 3 minutes.
Pour evenly into 3 - 9" greased cake pans. Bake at 350° for 20 - 25 minutes.
Ice with following caramel icing when cooled.

Caramel Icing

Use recipe for 'Creamy Caramels' on page 211. Follow directions until the boiling time; boil for 5 minutes only. Cool and add 1 1/2 cups powdered sugar and mix well.

This is just the right amount of icing for a 3 layer cake. If you don't want to make the layer cake from scratch, the Duncan Hines Butter Recipe cake mix is the one I like to use with this icing. This icing has a little different consistency than traditional icing, but it has always been a great hit wherever I take this cake!

    -Marti

Low Fat Sour Cream Pound Cake with Raspberry Sauce

1 reduced fat yellow cake mix
1/2 cup sugar
1 (8 oz.) container fat free sour
  cream
1 cup egg substitute
3/4 cup applesauce
1 tsp. vanilla extract

Place all ingredients into a large mixing bowl and beat on medium speed for 4 minutes.
Spoon batter into greased tube pan. Bake at 325° for 45 minutes or until a wooden pick inserted into center comes out clean. Cool in pan for 10 minutes; turn out onto serving plate.
Serve with raspberry sauce.

Raspberry sauce:
4 (10 oz.) pkgs. frozen
  raspberries, thawed
4 tsp. sugar

Process the berries and sugar in a blender or food processor until smooth. Pour through a strainer and discard seeds.
Chill for 1 hour.

Makes 16 servings.

-Ruth

Cream-Filled Coffeecake

An overnight recipe

1 cup milk

Heat milk to scalding; pour into a medium-sized mixing bowl.
Add the sugar, butter and salt and mix well.

1/2 cup sugar
1/2 cup butter, softened
1 tsp. salt
2 eggs, beaten

Add the eggs and mix well.

1 Tbsp. yeast
1/4 cup warm water
3 1/2 cups flour

Dissolve yeast in the warm water; let set 3 - 5 minutes. Add the above mixture.
Add the flour and mix well. Dough will be very sticky.
Place in a covered bowl and set in refrigerator overnight.
Combine all crumb ingredients and mix until crumbly. Set aside for use in the morning.

Crumbs:
1/2 cup brown sugar
1/2 cup flour
1/4 cup butter, softened
1 tsp. cinnamon

Filling:
1 1/2 Tbsp. flour
1 cup milk

The next morning; knead dough and divide into 3 greased 5"x8" pans.
Divide the crumbs evenly over the 3 pans.
Set aside and let rise until double in size, approximately 30 - 45 minutes.
Bake at 325° for 15 - 20 minutes.
Remove and cool completely.

1/2 cup sugar

1 cup shortening
1 tsp. vanilla
2 1/2 cups powdered sugar

Meanwhile combine the filling ingredients as follows;
Cook the flour and milk till thick.
Remove from heat; add sugar and mix well; cool.
Add the shortening, vanilla, powdered sugar and mix well.

My thanks to Mrs. Rueben (Elva) Kaufman for sharing this recipe many years ago while Jonas and I were weekend guests at their house.

Remove cakes from pans and split each cake horizontally. Divide filling evenly between the 3 cakes and replace tops

-Ruth

Banana Cupcakes

1/2 cup butter flavored shortening 1 cup sugar	*Cream shortening and sugar together.*
2 eggs	*Add eggs and beat well.*
1/2 tsp. baking soda 1 Tbsp. warm water	*Dissolve soda in warm water.*
1 cup bananas, mashed 1 tsp. vanilla	*Add the bananas, vanilla and dissolved soda; mix.*
1 2/3 cups flour 1/2 tsp. salt 1 tsp. baking powder 1 cup chopped nuts, optional	*Sift the dry ingredients; add to the creamed mixture.*
	Spoon into muffin tins that have been lined with cupcake papers. Bake at 350° for 15 minutes. Cool.

Cream Cheese Icing:
4 oz. cream cheese, softened
1/4 cup butter, softened
1/2 tsp. vanilla
1/2 lb. powdered sugar

Cream the cream cheese and butter together.
Add vanilla and powdered sugar and beat until smooth and creamy. Spread this icing evenly over the cupcakes. May sprinkle with chopped nuts.

Makes 20 - 24 cupcakes.

-Hannah

Black Bottom Cupcakes

1 1/2 cups flour
1 cup sugar
1/4 cup cocoa
1 tsp. baking soda
1/2 tsp. salt

Combine the dry ingredients in a large mixing bowl.

1 cup water
1/3 cup canola oil
1 Tbsp. white vinegar
1 tsp. vanilla

Gradually add the wet ingredients and mix until well blended. Place paper liners in muffin tins and fill cups 2/3 full with this mixture.

1 (8 oz.) pkg. cream cheese,
   softened
1 egg
1/3 cup sugar
1/8 tsp. salt
1 cup chocolate chips

Blend the cream cheese, egg, salt and sugar; gently stir in chocolate chips.

1/2 cup almond slivers
1/4 cup sugar

Drop 1 tablespoon of this mixture into the cups filled with chocolate mixture.

Sprinkle the almond slivers and sugar over each cupcake then bake at 350° for 35 minutes.

-Carolyn

Pumpkin Roll

3 eggs
1 cup sugar

Whip eggs and sugar until light and fluffy.

3/4 cup flour
1 tsp. baking powder
1/4 tsp. salt
1 tsp. cinnamon
1 tsp. pumpkin pie spice

Combine dry ingredients and fold into the creamed mixture.

3/4 cup pumpkin

Fold in pumpkin.

Pour batter into a greased jellyroll pan (11"x15"), that has been lined with waxed paper. Bake at 325° for 15 - 20 minutes

1/2 cup powdered sugar

Sprinkle powdered sugar over a slightly damp kitchen towel or cloth and turn warm cake out onto towel. Remove waxed paper; roll up, starting at long side of cake. Cool.

Filling:
1 (8 oz.) pkg. cream cheese, softened
1/2 cup powdered sugar
2 cups whipped topping
1 tsp. cinnamon

Combine the cream cheese and whipped topping and cream until smooth; add powdered sugar and cinnamon, beating well.
Unroll cake and 'ice' evenly with the filling mixture.
Roll up again, this time leaving towel off.

Option: this can be iced with cream cheese icing and sprinkled with chopped nuts or dusted with powdered sugar.

Top with icing or powdered sugar; slice and serve.

-Mom

Strawberry Cream Roll

4 eggs
1 tsp. vanilla extract

3/4 cup sugar

In a medium mixing bowl, beat eggs and vanilla on high speed for 5 minutes.
Gradually add the sugar, beating until dissolved.

3/4 cup cake flour
1 tsp. baking powder
1/4 tsp. salt

1/4 cup powdered sugar

Combine the dry ingredients; fold gently into the egg mixture, mixing just until combined.
Pour into a greased and waxed paper lined jelly-roll pan.
Bake at 375° for 10 - 12 minutes or until wooden pick inserted in center comes out clean.

Turn cake out onto a clean kitchen towel or cloth that has been sprinkled with the powdered sugar. Remove waxed paper; roll up cake and cloth. Cool.

Cream Filling:
1 cup whipping cream
1/4 cup sugar
1/2 tsp. vanilla extract
2 cups strawberries, sliced

White icing or
Whipped topping

Whole strawberries

Whip the cream; add the sugar and vanilla extract. Mix well.

Unroll cake; sprinkle the strawberries evenly over cake; spread with the cream filling.

Roll the cake again, without the cloth; chill.

Top with white icing or whipped topping and garnish with the strawberries.
Slice and serve.
Serves 10.

-Mom

Chocolate Ice Cream Roll

1/2 cup cake flour
1 tsp. baking powder
1/4 tsp. salt
1/3 cup cocoa

4 eggs, separated at room
    temperature

egg whites
1/4 cup sugar

egg yolks
1/2 cup sugar

cocoa

2 pints vanilla ice cream,
    softened

This is delicious
served with warm
cherry pie filling
or fresh fruit.

*Preheat oven to 375°. Grease a
15 1/2"x10 1/2" jellyroll pan; line
with waxed paper.*

*Combine the dry ingredients in a
small bowl and set aside.*

*Separate the eggs; place the yolks
into a large mixing bowl; set aside.
Place the egg whites in a small
mixing bowl; beat whites at high
speed until soft peaks form;
continue beating and gradually add
the sugar, beating until sugar is
completely dissolved. (Whites should
stand in stiff, glossy peaks.)*

*In a separate bowl with same
beaters, beat the egg yolks and sugar
until very thick.
Fold the flour mixture and egg white
mixture gently into the yolks with a
wire whisk.
Spread batter evenly into prepared
pan. Bake 12 - 14 minutes or until
cake springs back when touched
lightly with finger.
Sprinkle a clean cloth lightly with
cocoa. Invert cake onto cloth.
Remove waxed paper. Starting at
long end; roll cake up with towel.
Cool.
Unroll cake, spread ice cream evenly
over cake. Roll cake again without
cloth.
Wrap cake tightly with foil and
freeze until firm, about 3 hours.*

-Ruth

Chocolate Cheesecake

2 cups crushed chocolate
   sandwich cookies *or*
   graham cracker crumbs
5 Tbsp. butter, melted

Mix together the chocolate crumbs and melted butter until well blended. Press into a 9" springform pan.

3 pkgs. (8 oz.) cream cheese, at
   room temperature
1 cup sugar
5 large eggs
1/4 cup semi-sweet miniature
   chocolate chips

In a large mixing bowl, beat together the cream cheese, sugar and eggs until smooth and fluffy.
Stir in the chocolate chips. Pour the cream cheese mixture over the crust. Bake at 300° for 1 hour and 15 minutes.
Remove from oven and cool completely. Cover and chill for 2 hours.
Carefully remove the side of the springform pan.

2 cups milk chocolate chips,
   melted
1 cup sour cream

In a small bowl, mix together the sour cream and melted chocolate chips. Spread over the chilled cheesecake.
Chill briefly until frosting is set.

-Marti

Blueberry Swirl Cheesecake

2 (8 oz.) pkgs. cream cheese,
softened
1/2 cup sugar
1/4 tsp. vanilla

Beat together the cream cheese, sugar and vanilla until smooth and creamy.

2 eggs

Add the eggs and mix well.

1 - 9" prepared graham cracker
crust

Pour the cream mixture into the prepared pie shell.

1 can (21 oz.) blueberry pie
filling (any pie filling
flavor can be used.)

Spoon 1/3 of the the filling over the cream cheese filling; gently swirl into cheesecake with a spoon.

Bake at 350° for 40 minutes or until center is set. Cool to room temperature and then refrigerate. Serve with remaining topping, if desired.

-Marti

Old Fashioned Strawberry Shortcake

This recipe came from a friend, Bev Weaver. It was handed down to her from her grandmother, who got it from her mother, etc. It truly is old-fashioned!

1/4 cup sugar
1/2 cup shortening
1 egg

Cream sugar and shortening together; add egg and mix well.

1/2 tsp. salt
2 cups flour
4 tsp. baking powder
1 cup milk

Combine the dry ingredients and add alternately with the milk to the creamed mixture. Mix just until well blended. Do not overmix.

Fresh strawberries, sliced and sweetened
whipped cream or milk

Place batter into a greased 9"x9" pan, bake at 350° for 30 minutes. Cool slightly, cut into squares and top individual squares with strawberries and cream.

This recipe can be doubled in size; baked in 3 - 9" round pans. Then prepare a 3 layer shortcake by starting with 1 layer, topping with whipped cream, then a layer of sweetened strawberries and repeating this till all cake layers are used. Finish with cream and strawberries and top with a whole berry, still capped for garnish. Makes a beautiful dessert!

-Carolyn

Apple Dumplings in Sauce

2 cups flour
1/4 tsp. salt
1/2 cup butter, softened

2/3 cup sour cream

6 medium Granny Smith apples,
   peeled and cored

1/2 cup sugar
1 1/2 tsp. cinnamon
2 Tbsp. butter, softened

milk

Sauce:
1/2 cup brown sugar, firmly
   packed
2 Tbsp. butter
1/2 cup whipping cream
1 Tbsp. vanilla

Makes 6 servings.

In a medium bowl, stir together the flour and salt. Cut in the butter until mixture forms coarse crumbs.

With a fork, stir in the sour cream; mix until it forms a ball.
On a lightly floured surface, roll the dough to a 12"x18" rectangle. Cut into 6 - 6" squares. Place an apple in the center of each square.

In a small bowl, stir together the sugar, butter and cinnamon. Stuff 1 1/2 Tbsp. into cored center of each apple. Fold the dough up around each apple; seal seams.
Place seam side down on a greased 15"x10" jellyroll pan. Brush dough with milk and prick it with a fork. Bake for 35 - 45 minutes or until apples are tender.

Combine all sauce ingredients in a 1-quart saucepan. Cook over medium heat until mixture comes to a full boil. Serve sauce over warm dumplings.

Option: Cut leaf designs out of the dough scraps; place one or two leaves on top of each wrapped apple.

-Ruth

Old Fashioned Apple Roll-Ups

1 1/4 cups brown sugar
1 cup water
1/2 cup butter
1/2 tsp. cinnamon

Combine these ingredients in a small saucepan; stir and heat till butter is melted and sugar is dissolved. Set aside.

2 cups flour
2 1/2 tsp. baking powder
1/2 tsp. salt
2/3 cup shortening
1/2 cup milk

Combine the flour, baking powder and salt, cut in shortening till mixture forms coarse crumbs.
Add milk, blending just until it forms a soft ball.
Roll out dough on a lightly floured surface to a 12"x18" rectangle.

6 medium sized tart apples, shredded just prior to use.

Sprinkle the shredded apples evenly over the surface of the dough.
Sprinkle cinnamon and sugar over the apples to your taste.
Begin rolling dough from long end of rectangle and roll tightly, ending with seam side down.
Slice into 1" - 1 1/2" pieces and place into a greased 9"x13" baking dish.
Pour reserved sauce over the roll-ups and bake at 350° for 35 - 40 minutes until dough part of roll-ups are golden brown.

Serve warm with ice cream.

-Carolyn

Chocolate Ice-Cream Brownies

1 (23.6 oz.) pkg. fudge brownie
  mix

Prepare brownie mix according to directions on package. Spread onto a lightly greased 9"x13" pan. Bake and cool.

1/2 gallon vanilla ice cream,
  softened

Spread ice cream over the cooled brownies; freeze until hardened.

2 cups powdered sugar, sifted
2/3 cups semi-sweet chocolate
  chips
1 1/2 cups evaporated milk
1/2 cup butter or margarine

Combine the next 4 ingredients in a small saucepan; bring to a boil. Reduce heat to medium and cook for 8 minutes. Remove from heat; stir in vanilla and nuts. Cool. Spread over ice cream. Freeze.

1 tsp. vanilla extract
1 1/2 cups chopped nuts

Remove from freezer 5 - 10 minutes prior to serving. Cut into squares.

Serve 12 - 15.

-Hannah

Buster Bar Dessert

25 chocolate sandwich cookies,
    crushed
1/4 cup butter

Combine the crushed cookies and butter. Press into a 9"x13" pan. Chill.

1/2 gallon vanilla ice cream,
    softened
1 1/2 cup Spanish peanuts

Spread ice cream over chilled crust. Sprinkle with the peanuts. Freeze.

1 cup chocolate chips
2 cups powdered sugar
1/2 cup butter
1 1/4 cups evaporated milk

Place these 4 ingredients into a medium-sized saucepan; bring to a boil. Boil on medium heat for 8 minutes. Remove from heat and spread evenly over the ice cream and peanuts.
Freeze until firm.

8 oz. whipped topping

Frost with whipped topping. Cut into squares and serve.

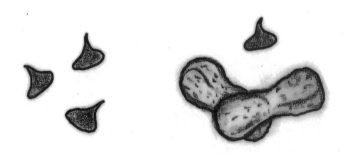

Prepare this easy dessert several days ahead for a no fuss company meal.

-Kathleen

Fudgey
Ice Cream Dessert

20 chocolate sandwich cookies
1/4 cup butter, melted

Crush the cookies; add butter and combine. Press into a 9"x13" pan.

1/2 gallon vanilla *or* chocolate
  chip ice cream, softened

Slice or spoon ice cream over the cookie crust. Place in freezer while you prepare the sauce.

4 oz. squares German sweet
  chocolate
1/2 cup semi-sweet chocolate chips
2/3 cup evaporated milk
1/2 tsp. salt
2/3 cup sugar
1/2 cup butter
1 tsp. vanilla extract

Combine the next 6 ingredients in a medium saucepan; boil for 4 minutes while stirring constantly. Remove from heat, add vanilla and cool.
When cooled to room temperature, pour over the ice cream. Return to freezer.

8 oz. whipped topping
chopped pecans

When ready to serve, top with the whipped topping and sprinkle with pecans.

-Carolyn

Mississippi Mud Pie

1 lb. oreo cookies
1/4 cup butter, melted

Crush the oreos; add melted butter and combine. Press into a 9" deep dish pie plate. Freeze.

1/2 gallon coffee flavored ice cream

Spoon the softened ice cream over the crust; pour the hot fudge sauce over the ice cream.
Sprinkle with chopped walnuts and freeze until ready to serve.

hot fudge sauce
chopped walnuts*

*may substitute toasted almonds

Let set at room temperature for 10 minutes before serving.

My thanks to Sandy Torres for sharing this recipe! Our families have enjoyed sharing lots of meals together, and we always look forward to her rich and delicious desserts.

-Ruth

Butterscotch Ice Cream Pudding

50 Ritz crackers, crushed
1/2 cup butter, melted

Mix crackers and butter together. Set aside 1/2 cup; press remaining crumbs into a 13"x9" pan.

1 box (3.9 oz.) instant vanilla
    pudding
1 box (3.9 oz.) instant butter
    scotch pudding
1 1/2 cups cold milk

Combine these ingredients in a large mixing bowl and beat well. Let stand for 5 - 10 minutes.

1/2 gallon ice cream, softened

Add ice cream to the pudding mixture and mix well.
Pour this over the crust. Sprinkle remaining 1/2 cup of crumbs on top.
Freeze.

Remove from freezer 15 - 20 minutes before serving and cut into squares.

Serves 15 - 20.

This recipe was given by a friend, Anna Ruth Kauffman, from Ohio. Jonas and I went to visit them one summer and we'll always remember the good time we had sitting in their kitchen, enjoying this delectable dessert while chatting about 'old times' with her and her husband Mark.

-Ruth

Graham Cracker Jello Dessert

2 cups graham cracker crumbs
3 Tbsp. sugar
1/3 cup butter, melted

Mix the crumbs, sugar and butter together thoroughly. Reserve 1/2 cup of crumbs for top. Press remaining crumbs into a 9"x13" pan.

1 (3 oz.) box raspberry gelatin
1 cup boiling water

Dissolve gelatin in boiling water. Chill until partially set. Whip until foamy. Set aside.

1 (12 oz.) can evaporated milk, chilled

Whip the chilled evaporated milk in a large mixing bowl. Set aside.

1 (8 oz.) pkg. cream cheese, softened
1 cup sugar
1 tsp. vanilla

Cream the next 3 ingredients together. Blend into the evaporated milk.

Fold the gelatin into the cream cheese mixture.

Pour into graham cracker crust. Top with reserved 1/2 cup crumbs.

Chill at least 1 hour before serving.

Our family enjoys this as a light dessert after a large holiday meal.

-Kathleen

Strawberry-Rhubarb Tapioca

2 cups chopped rhubarb
1/4 cup minute tapioca
3/4 cup sugar
2 cups water

Combine the first 4 ingredients in a medium saucepan and cook until clear. Remove from heat.

2 Tbsp. strawberry gelatin
2 cups strawberries, sliced

Add these ingredients to the above mixture.

whipped cream

Chill and serve with the whipped cream.

Serves 6.

-Kathleen

Lemon Pudding

1/2 cup butter, melted
1 1/2 cup flour
3/4 cup chopped pecans

Combine the first 3 ingredients and press into a 9"x13" pan. Bake at 325° for 10 - 12 minutes or until lightly browned. Cool.

1 (8 oz.) cream cheese, softened
1 cup powdered sugar
1 cup whipping cream

Combine the next 3 ingredients and blend until smooth and creamy. Spread over cooled crust.

2 small (3.9 oz.) boxes instant
   lemon pudding
3 cups milk

Mix 2 boxes pudding mix with the 3 cups milk. Pour over the cream cheese mixture.

whipped topping, optional

If desired, top with whipped topping; cut into squares and serve.

When I was a new bride, mom put together a box of recipes collected from my relatives to help me get started cooking. This is one from a cousin, Mary Lou Miller, that we have enjoyed greatly over the years.

-Ruth

Strawberry Delight

Bottom Layer:
2 pkgs. graham cracker, crushed
1/2 cup butter, melted

Combine the crackers and butter; press into a 9"x13" pan.

Center:
1 (8 oz.) pkg. cream cheese, softened
1 (14 oz.) can Eagle brand sweetened condensed milk
1/3 cup lemon juice
1 tsp. vanilla extract

Place cream cheese in medium-sized mixing bowl; beat until smooth. Add the milk and continue whipping till light and fluffy. Add the lemon and vanilla.
Spoon this mixture over the crust and let set in refrigerator for 2 - 3 hours.

Top Layer:
1 3/4 cup water
1/4 cup clear jel or cornstarch
1/2 cup sugar

1 Tbsp. strawberry gelatin

Place the water, sugar and clear jel into a medium-sized saucepan. Bring to a boil and cook until thickened.
Remove from the heat and add the gelatin, stirring till well blended.

1 - 1 1/2 quarts fresh strawberries, sliced

Add the strawberries and pour over the cream cheese mixture.
Chill and serve.

-Ruth

Creme Brulee'

3 cups heavy cream
dash of salt

In a medium saucepan, combine the cream and salt; cook over medium heat until it simmers. Do not boil. Remove from heat.

6 egg yolks
2/3 cup granulated sugar

In a mixing bowl, combine egg yolks and sugar; stir well. Gradually add to the cream, stirring until sugar dissolves.

1 tsp. vanilla

Stir in the vanilla.

Strain mixture into a large glass measuring cup.

Fill 6 oven proof custard cups (6 - 8 oz. each) with the mixture and place them in a large roasting pan.

Place in hot oven and pour hot water into the roasting pan halfway up the sides of the custard cups.

Cover loosely with foil.

Bake at 300° for 1 hour and 15 minutes, or until set.

Remove; cool. Chill for several hours or overnight.

Before serving; preheat broiler for 10 minutes. Sprinkle 1 Tbsp. brown sugar evenly over each cup.

6 Tbsp. brown sugar

Caramelize sugar by placing custard cups, a few at a time as close to the broiler as possible. This will take only 30 seconds to a minute, so watch carefully! Refrigerate if not serving immediately.

Do not refrigerate for more than 3 - 4 hours after caramelizing sugar as it will cause the sugar to liquefy.

This a creamy custard topped with burnt sugar. The name is French and translates as burnt cream.
An impressive dessert to serve!

Serves 6.

-Ruth

Pineapple Cheese Torte

Crust:
1 1/2 cup flour
1/2 cup sugar
3/4 cup nuts, chopped
3/4 cup butter, melted

Combine crust ingredients; pat into a 8"x12" pan.
Bake at 350° for 10 minutes or until lightly browned.

Filling:
2 (8 oz.) pkgs. cream cheese, softened
1/2 cup sugar
2 eggs
2/3 cup unsweetened pineapple juice*

Beat the cream cheese in mixing bowl until fluffy; add sugar and eggs, beating well. Beat in juice on low speed just until blended.
Pour filling over hot crust. Bake at 350° for 18 - 20 minutes or until center is set. Cool.

Topping:
1/4 cup flour
1/4 cup sugar
1 (20 oz.) can crushed pineapple, drained, juice reserved
1 cup unsweetened pineapple juice*
1/2 cup whipping cream

Whipped topping for garnish, optional

Combine flour and sugar in a small saucepan. With a small whisk stir in the pineapple juice. Bring to a boil, stirring constantly. Boil for 1 minute. Remove from heat and fold in the drained pineapple.Cool.
Whip the cream until stiff peaks form; fold into topping and spread over dessert.
Refrigerate 6 hours or overnight. Garnish with whipped topping.
Serves 12 - 14.

*The reserved juice from the pineapple can be used, but it will not be enough to make up the 1 2/3 cup you will need for the whole recipe. If only a small amount is needed you may add orange juice or water, otherwise pineapple juice can be purchased in 6 oz. cans to make up the difference.

Note: this dessert is best if made the day ahead!

-Hannah

Cookies,
Bars,
and
Candies

COOKIES, BARS AND CANDIES

Grandma's Tea Cakes

1 cup shortening
1 1/2 cups sugar

Cream the shortening; gradually add sugar, beating well at moderate speed.

3 eggs

Add eggs, one at a time, beating well after each addition.

4 cups flour
2 tsp. baking powder
1 tsp. baking soda
1/2 tsp. salt
1/4 cup buttermilk

Combine the dry ingredients and add to the creamed mixture alternately with the buttermilk. Mix well.

1 1/4 tsp. almond extract

Add the extract.

Sugar

Drop by teaspoonful onto a greased cookie sheet.
Sprinkle with sugar and bake at 350° for 12 - 15 minutes.

Makes 4 dozen cookies.

-Mom

Soft Sugar Cookies

2 cups sugar
1 cup shortening

Cream sugar and shortening in large mixing bowl.

2 eggs

Add eggs, one at a time, mix well.

4 1/2 cups flour
1 1/2 tsp. soda
2 tsp. baking powder
2 tsp. cream of tarter
1 tsp. salt
1 cup milk
1 1/2 tsp. vanilla

Add the dry ingredients alternately with the milk; add vanilla.

Cookies may be dropped by teaspoonful onto greased baking sheet or rolled to 1/4" thickness and cut with cookie cutters.
If you cut out cookies, sprinkle lots of flour on hard surface and use generously on dough as you roll it out for easy handling.

Bake at 350° for 10 minutes or until delicately browned.

-Ruth

Soft Butter Cookies

We sell a lot of these cookies at Sugar N' Spice.

1 cup butter
2 cups sugar

Cream butter and sugar together in a large mixing bowl.

3 eggs

Add the eggs and continue beating until light and fluffy.

1 cup sour cream
2 tsp. vanilla
1 tsp. baking soda
1/2 tsp. salt
4 1/2 cups flour

Add the remaining ingredients and mix well.

Chill.
Drop by teaspoonful onto an ungreased cookie sheet. Bake for 10 - 15 minutes.

Caramel Icing:

Cool and ice with caramel icing.

3 cups powdered sugar
3/4 cup shortening
3/4 cup caramel topping

Combine all icing ingredients and beat until smooth and creamy. Spread over the butter cookies.

Sugar 'n Spice
Bake Shop

-Mom

Whoopie Pies

A Marshmallow Creme Filled Chocolate Cookie

1 cup shortening
2 cups sugar
2 eggs

Cream shortening and sugar together. Add the eggs, beating well after each one.

4 cups flour
2 tsp. soda
1 tsp. salt
1 cup cocoa
1 cup hot water
1 cup sour milk*
2 tsp. vanilla extract

Add the dry ingredients alternating with the water and milk. Mix well and add the vanilla.

Drop by spoonful onto cookie sheets. Bake at 400° for 8 minutes.

Filling:
3/4 cup butter, softened
2 cups powdered sugar
2 (7 oz.) jars marshmallow creme
1 tsp. vanilla extract

In a large mixing bowl beat the butter until smooth. Add the powdered sugar. Then beat in marshmallow creme and vanilla. Beat until smooth.

*to make sour milk use 1 Tbsp. vinegar and enough milk to equal one cup.

Spread the filling over a cooled cookie and top with another cookie. Wrap each one individually with plastic wrap.

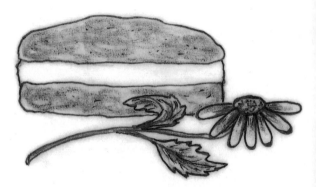

-Ruth

Chocolate Chip Oatmeal Sandwich Cookie

1 cup butter, softened
1 1/4 cups brown sugar
1/2 cup sugar

Combine the butter and sugars; mix until creamy.

2 eggs
2 Tbsp. milk
2 tsp. vanilla

Add the eggs, vanilla and milk to the creamed mixture and mix well.

1 3/4 cups flour
2 tsp. soda
1/2 tsp. salt
1/2 tsp. cinnamon

Sift these ingredients and add to the above mixture; mix well.

2 1/2 cups quick oats
1 (12 oz.) pkg. miniature
   chocolate chips
1/2 cup chopped nuts, optional

Stir in oats, chocolate chips and nuts.
Drop by rounded tablespoonful onto greased cookie sheets.
Bake at 350° for 9 - 10 minutes.
Let cool. Spread the following filling recipe over a cookie and top with another. Wrap each cookie individually.

Filling:
1/4 cup water
1 1/2 tsp. plain gelatin

Dissolve the gelatin in the water; let set for 5 minutes, then place in microwave for 30 seconds or till completely dissolved.

1 lb powdered sugar
3/4 cup shortening
1/4 tsp. vanilla

Place the water, sugar, shortening and vanilla into a large mixing bowl and beat until smooth and creamy.
Add more water if needed for spreadable consistency.

-Carolyn

Chocolate Chip Cookies

Ruth's Version

2 1/8 cups brown sugar
1 cup white sugar
2 cups shortening

6 eggs

7 cups flour
2 tsp. salt
4 tsp. soda
4 tsp. cream of tarter

1 3/4 cup chocolate chips
1 Tbsp. vanilla extract

Cream sugars and shortening together.

Add eggs to the creamed mixture, mixing well.

Add the dry ingredients and mix well.

Add the chocolate chips and vanilla.

Drop by teaspoonful onto baking trays.
Bake at 375° for 10 - 12 minutes.

Marti's version

1/2 cup butter, softened
1/2 cup shortening, butter flavor
1/2 cup cream cheese, softened

3/4 cup sugar
3/4 cup brown sugar
1 tsp. vanilla
2 eggs
1 tsp. baking soda
1/2 tsp. salt

3 cups flour

2 cups chocolate chips
1 cup pecans, optional

Combine the butter, shortening and cream cheese, mixing until creamy.

Add the next 6 ingredients and mix on medium speed for 4 minutes.

Add the flour; mix well.

Stir in the chocolate chips and pecans.
Drop by teaspoonful onto baking sheet and bake at 350° for 10 minutes.

Chocolate Peanut Butter Cookies

No Bake!

2 cups sugar
1/2 cup milk
1/2 cup butter
3 Tbsp. cocoa

Combine the first 4 ingredients in a medium saucepan. Bring to a boil, stirring until dissolved. Boil for 2 minutes. Remove from heat.

1/2 cup crunchy peanut butter
1 tsp. vanilla extract
3 1/2 cups quick oatmeal

Stir in the peanut butter, vanilla and oatmeal until well mixed. Drop by spoonfuls onto waxed paper or baking sheet.

Let cool till firm.

Makes 4 - 5 dozen

Even though I am the only boy in our family, the girls still tell me to make these cookies.

-Kevin

Peanut Butter Cookies

1 1/2 cups crunchy peanut
    butter
1/2 cup butter shortening
1/2 cup butter
1 1/4 cups brown sugar
1 1/4 cups white sugar
6 Tbsp. milk
2 tsp. vanilla

Combine the first 7 ingredients and mix until creamy.

2 eggs

Add the eggs and mix just until blended.

3 1/2 cups flour
1 1/2 tsp. salt
1 1/2 tsp. soda

Combine the dry ingredients in a small bowl. Gradually add to the creamed mixture. Mix only until blended; do not overbeat!

granulated sugar
Hershey kisses

Shape into 1" balls and roll in sugar. Place on a baking sheet and flatten slightly with cup and top with a Hershey kiss.

Bake at 350° for 10 - 12 minutes.

These cookies are delicious and don't last long around our house!

-Janelle

Peanut Butter Oatmeal Cookies

1 cup shortening, butter flavor
1 cup brown sugar
3/4 cup white sugar
2 eggs

Cream shortening and sugars together; add eggs and whip until light and fluffy.

1 cup peanut butter

Add peanut butter and mix again.

2 cups flour
2 tsp. soda
1/2 tsp. salt

Sift dry ingredients and add to mixture.

1 cup quick oats

Stir in oats.

Form into approximately 2 1/2" thick logs and refrigerate several hours or overnight.
Remove from refrigerator and slice.
Place slices on baking sheet.
Bake at 350° for 8 - 9 minutes.

-Hannah

Oatmeal Cookies

1 cup white sugar
1 cup brown sugar
1 cup shortening

Cream sugars and shortening together until light and fluffy.

2 eggs

Add eggs to the creamed mixture and continue beating.

2 cups flour
1 1/2 cups quick oats
1 tsp. baking soda
2 tsp. baking powder
3/4 tsp. salt

Add the dry ingredients and mix well.

1 tsp. vanilla extract
2 Tbsp. water

Add vanilla and water.
Drop by tablespoonful onto baking trays; flatten slightly and bake at 325° for 10 - 12 minutes.

When the children were small, they used to call these cookies 'Cave Cookies' because of the cavern-like holes throughout the cookie. It was one of their favorites!

-Mom

Toasted Oat Coconut Cookies

The coconut extract, rice krispies and pan toasted oats in this recipe makes this a unique tasting cookie that is chewy, yet crispy!

1/4 cup butter, softened
1/4 cup shortening
1 cup sugar

Cream butter and shortening; add sugar and beat until light and fluffy.

1 egg
1/2 tsp. coconut extract

Add the egg and extract; beat well.

1 1/2 cups flour
1 tsp. baking powder
1/2 tsp. baking soda
1/2 tsp. salt

Combine these 4 dry ingredients. Gradually add to creamed mixture; mix well.

1 cup flaked coconut
1/2 cup crispy rice cereal
1/2 cup regular oats, (pan
   toasted under broiler)

Stir in the coconut, cereal and toasted oats.

Shape into 1" balls; place on baking sheets.
Bake at 325° for 12 - 14 minutes or until golden.

Makes 4 dozen cookies.

-Ruth

Molasses Crinkles

3/4 cup shortening
1 cup brown sugar

Cream shortening and sugar together.

1 egg
1/4 cup molasses, *or* dark corn
    syrup

Add egg and molasses and beat until well blended.

2 1/4 cups flour
1/2 tsp. salt
2 tsp. soda
1 tsp. cinnamon
1 tsp. ginger
1/2 tsp. cloves

Combine the dry ingredients and add to creamed mixture. Mix thoroughly.

Chill dough in refrigerator.

1/8 - 1/2 cup granulated sugar

Shape the chilled dough into 1" balls. Roll in the granulated sugar and place 2" apart on baking sheet.

Bake at 350° for 12 - 15 minutes.

Makes 4 dozen cookies.

-Ruth

Spiced Cookies

2 cups brown sugar
1 cup shortening, butter flavored

Cream shortening and sugar together.

1 1/4 cups milk
3 eggs
1 tsp. vanilla extract

Add milk, eggs and vanilla and mix well.

4 cups flour
2 tsp. baking soda
2 tsp. baking powder
1 tsp. cinnamon
1/4 tsp. cloves
1 tsp. salt

Sift all dry ingredients and add to mixture, beating well.

Drop by teaspoonful onto a greased baking tray.
Bake at 350° for 10 minutes.
Cool slightly then spread with following icing.

Icing:
6 Tbsp. butter
3 Tbsp. hot water
1 tsp. vanilla extract
powdered sugar

Melt butter; add water and vanilla. Mix in powdered sugar, adding till icing is thick enough to spread.

-Hannah

Snickerdoodles

1 cup butter
1 1/2 cups sugar

Cream butter and sugar together.

2 eggs

Add the eggs and blend well.

2 3/4 cups flour
2 tsp. cream of tarter
1 tsp. baking powder
1/4 tsp. salt

In a separate bowl, combine the dry ingredients.
Add to the creamed mixture and mix well.

3 Tbsp. sugar
1 tsp. cinnamon

In a shallow bowl, stir together the sugar and cinnamon.

Shape the dough into 1" balls and roll in the sugar mixture.
Bake at 350° for 8 - 10 minutes.

Makes about 5 dozen cookies.

-Ruth

Monster Cookies

3 eggs
1 cup white sugar
1 cup brown sugar
1/2 cup butter, softened

Cream the eggs, sugars and butter until light and fluffy.

1 tsp. vanilla
1 tsp. corn syrup
1 1/2 cups crunchy peanut
    butter
2 tsp. baking soda

Add the next 4 ingredients and mix well.

1 cup flour
3 1/2 cups quick oatmeal

Gradually add the flour and oats, mixing well.

2/3 cup chocolate chips
1/2 lb. peanut M&M's
1/2 lb. plain M&M's

Stir in the chocolate chips and M&M's.

Drop by teaspoonful onto a greased cookie sheet.

Bake at 350° for 10 - 12 minutes. Do not overbake!

-Krystal

Cherry Chocolate Kisses

2 cups butter, softened
2 cups powdered sugar
4 tsp. maraschino cherry juice
1 tsp. almond extract
few drops red food coloring

Combine the first 5 ingredients.
Blend well.

4 1/2 cups flour
1 tsp. salt

Stir in the flour and salt.

1 cup maraschino cherries,
   drained and chopped

Add cherries and mix well.
Form dough into 1" balls. Place 2"
apart on baking sheet.

96 chocolate kisses, unwrapped

Bake at 350° for 8 - 10 minutes or
until lightly browned around edges.
Remove from oven and immediately
top each cookie with a chocolate
kiss then remove from baking sheet.

Makes 8 dozen cookies.

This is a delicious cookie if you enjoy maraschino
cherries and chocolate kisses!

-Mom

Butter Crisps

A cookie press recipe

1 cup butter
1 (3 oz.) pkg. cream cheese,
   softened
1 cup sugar

Cream the butter and cream cheese. Add sugar gradually and beat until light and fluffy.

1 egg yolk
1 tsp. vanilla

Beat in egg yolk and vanilla.

2 1/4 cups flour
1/2 tsp. salt
1/4 tsp. baking powder

Add the dry ingredients to the creamed mixture gradually.

Pack into a cookie press and press out onto baking sheet.

Bake at 350° for 12 - 15 minutes.

*Dough may be tinted with different colors before baking and sprinkled with colored sugars.

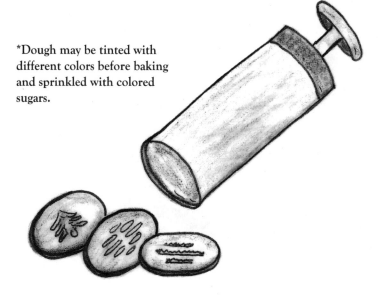

-Ruth

Nutty Cheese Bars

Preheat oven to 350°.

1 box Duncan Hines butter
   recipe cake mix
3/4 cup butter, melted
3/4 cup chopped pecans or
   walnuts

Topping:
1 cup packed brown sugar
2 (8 oz.) pkgs. cream cheese,
   softened

3/4 cup chopped pecans or
   walnuts

Grease and flour a 9"x13" baking pan.
In a medium-sized mixing bowl, stir together the dry cake mix, butter and nuts until well blended.
Press the mixture evenly into the baking pan.

Combine the brown sugar and cream cheese and stir with spoon until well mixed.
Spread this over the cake mixture in pan.

Top with nuts.
Bake at 350° for 25 - 30 minutes or until edges are browned and cheese topping is set.

Cool completely before cutting into bars.
Store in an airtight container in refrigerator.

For cream cheese lovers, these bars are a must!
-Hannah

202

Frosted Pumpkin Bars

4 eggs
1 cup vegetable oil
2 cups sugar

Beat eggs in a large mixing bowl.
Add oil and sugar; mix well.

1 cup pumpkin
1/2 tsp. salt
2 tsp. cinnamon
1 tsp. baking soda
1 tsp. baking powder
2 cups flour

Gradually add the remaining
ingredients and mix well.
Pour batter into a lightly greased
and floured 12"x18"x1" cookie
sheet.

Bake at 350° for 20 - 25 minutes.
Remove and cool then ice with
following icing.

Icing:
3 oz. cream cheese, softened
6 Tbsp. butter, softened
2 1/2 cups powdered sugar
1 tsp. vanilla
1 - 2 tsp. milk

Combine all icing ingredients and
mix until creamy.
Spread over the cooled bars.

This is another recipe from the collection that Mom
gathered for me from our relatives. Sue Ellen Hershberger,
Dad's niece, generously shared this recipe and it's one of
my favorites.

-Ruth

Banana Bars

1 1/2 cups sugar
1/2 cup butter, softened

Cream sugar and butter together.

2 eggs
1 cup sour cream

Add eggs and sour cream. Mix well.

3 large ripe bananas, mashed
2 tsp. vanilla extract

Add bananas and vanilla, mixing until well blended.

1 tsp. salt
1 tsp. baking soda
2 cups flour

Combine the dry ingredients and add to the banana mixture. Mix well.

Pour batter into a greased and floured jellyroll (10"x15") pan. Bake at 350° for 20 - 25 minutes.

Cream Cheese Icing:
3 oz. cream cheese, softened
6 Tbsp. butter, softened
2 cups powdered sugar
1 tsp. vanilla extract
1 Tbsp. milk

Combine all icing ingredients and beat until smooth and creamy. Spread over cooled bars.

-Carolyn

Zucchini-Carrot Bars

2 cups sugar
1 cup oil
3 eggs

Combine the sugar, oil and eggs in a large mixing bowl. Cream until light and fluffy.

2 cups flour
1 1/2 tsp. cinnamon
1 tsp. salt
1 tsp. baking soda
1 tsp. baking powder

Combine the dry ingredients and add to the creamed mixture gradually. Beat for 2 minutes.

1 tsp. vanilla extract
2 cups shredded zucchini
1 carrot, shredded
3/4 cup quick oats
1 cup chopped nuts, optional

Fold in the remaining ingredients. Pour batter into a greased jellyroll (15"x10") pan.
Bake at 350° for 40 - 45 minutes. Cool and ice with cream cheese icing (see recipe on page 204).

-Carolyn

One Bowl Brownies

4 (1 oz.) squares Bakers
    unsweetened chocolate
3/4 cup margarine

Melt chocolate and margarine in microwave or double boiler.

2 cups sugar

Stir sugar into the chocolate.

3 eggs
1 tsp. vanilla

Add eggs and vanilla; mix well.

1 cup flour
1 cup nuts

Add flour and nuts; mix in well.
Pour batter into a greased 9"x13" baking dish.
Bake at 350° for 30 - 35 minutes.
Cool in pan and cut into squares.

This is an easy way to get your children started baking!

-Hannah

Toffee Nut Bars

1 cup butter, softened
1 cup brown sugar
2 cups flour

Mix all ingredients until soft dough forms, may be slightly crumbly. Press firmly into an 11"x17" cookie sheet to form thin crust.

3 eggs
2 cups brown sugar
1 tsp. vanilla

Beat eggs well; add sugar and vanilla, mixing until light and fluffy.

2 Tbsp. flour
2 tsp. baking powder
1 tsp. salt

Add the next three dry ingredients and mix well.

1 1/2 cups coconut
1 cup chopped nuts
2 cups chocolate chips

Fold in the remaining ingredients. Pour batter over the crust and bake at 350° for 30 - 35 minutes, or until golden brown on top.

-Carolyn

Chocolate Butter Crisps

1 cup butter
1 cup brown sugar
1 egg yolk

Cream butter and sugar until light and fluffy.
Add egg yolk and continue mixing.

2 cups flour
1 tsp. vanilla

Add flour and vanilla, stirring just until well blended.

6 oz. milk chocolate chips
1 cup chopped pecans

Press into a jellyroll (10"x15") pan. Bake at 350° for 20 - 25 minutes. Remove from oven and sprinkle with the chocolate chips; when chips are softened from the heat, spread gently. Sprinkle pecans over chocolate layer. Slice while still warm!

-Carolyn

Cheesecake Cookie Bars

2/3 cup butter, melted
2/3 cup brown sugar
2 cups flour
1 cup chopped pecans

Combine the first 4 ingredients and mix until coarse crumbs form. Reserve 2/3 cup of crumbs and press remainder into a 9"x13" baking pan. Bake at 350° for 12 - 15 minutes.

2 (8 oz.) pkg. cream cheese, softened
1/2 cup sugar
2 eggs
4 Tbsp. milk
juice of 1 lemon *or*
    2 Tbsp. lemon juice
2 tsp. vanilla extract

Meanwhile prepare the filling; blend cream cheese and sugar together. Add remaining ingredients and mix until smooth.

Pour into baked crust. Sprinkle reserved crumbs evenly over the top and continue baking for an additional 15 - 20 minutes or until set.
Cool.

Fresh fruit for garnish, optional

Cut into squares, then cut diagonally to make a triangle shape. Garnish with fresh fruit.

-Ruth

Almond Brittle

1/4 cup butter

Melt butter in a 10" frying pan.

1 cup sliced almonds
1 Tbsp. light corn syrup
1/2 cup sugar

Add almonds, corn syrup and sugar all at once. Cook over medium heat; stir constantly. (5 - 6 minutes) until golden in color.

Immediately empty onto a piece of tin foil, spread as flat and fast as possible.

Cool. Break into pieces.

This recipe is from my sister-in-law Janette who lives in Oregon and is a fantastic cook. We've shared lots of recipes (and quilt patterns) over the years....   -Ruth

Buckeyes

1 lb. powdered sugar
1/2 cup butter
18 oz. peanut butter

Combine the sugar, butter and peanut butter; mix well.
Chill until firm enough to shape; then shape into 1" ball.
Chill again for 1 - 2 hours.

12 oz. pkg. chocolate chips
2 tsp. white shortening

Melt chocolate chips and shortening in microwave or double boiler. Use wooden pick to pick up peanut butter balls and to dip into melted chocolate.
Leave small area around toothpick uncovered to resemble a buckeye. Still with pick in place; place dipped peanut butter ball on a flat sheet lined with waxed paper. Remove toothpick and let set or chill till chocolate hardens.

-Carolyn

Three Chocolate Fudge

3 1/3 cups sugar
1 cup butter
1 cup packed brown sugar
1 (12 oz.) can evaporated milk

Combine the first 4 ingredients in a large saucepan. Cook and stir over medium heat until sugar is dissolved. Bring to a rapid boil; boil 5 minutes; stir constantly.

32 large marshmallows, halved

Add the marshmallows and stir until melted. Remove from heat.

2 cups chocolate chips

Add the chips and stir until melted.

2 (7 oz.) milk chocolate candy
   bars, broken
2 (1 oz.) squares semi-sweet
   baking squares

Add the bars and stir until melted.

1 tsp. vanilla extract
2 cups chopped nuts

Fold in remaining 2 ingredients; mix well.

Pour into a greased jellyroll (15"x10") pan.
Cool and cut into squares.

Makes 5 1/2 lbs.

-Marti

Chocolate Truffles

1 1/2 pkgs. (12 oz.) semi-sweet
   chocolate chips

Melt chocolate in microwave or double boiler. Set aside.

1 (8 oz.) pkg. cream cheese
3 cups powdered sugar
1 1/2 tsp. vanilla

Beat cream cheese until smooth. Gradually add sugar, beating until well blended. Add melted chocolate and vanilla. Mix well.

chopped nuts and/or
flaked coconut, toasted

Refrigerate 1 hour. Shape into 1" balls. Roll in nuts or coconut. Store in an airtight container in refrigerator.

Makes about 5 dozen truffles.

-Hannah

Mocha Truffles

2 (12 oz.) pkgs. semi-sweet
   chocolate chips

Melt chocolate chips in microwave or double boiler.

1 (8 oz.) pkg. cream cheese,
   softened
3 Tbsp. instant coffee granules
2 tsp. water

Add cream cheese, coffee and water to the chocolate mixture; mix well. Chill until firm enough to shape.

Shape into 1" balls and place on waxed paper lined baking sheet. Chill for 1 - 2 hours or until firm.

1 lb. dark (semi-sweet) chocolate
   for coating.

white coating chocolate, optional

Melt chocolate coating in microwave or double boiler. Dip balls and return to lined baking sheet to harden. If desired, melt the white chocolate and drizzle over coated balls.

-Marti

Creamy Caramels

1 cup sugar
1 cup dark corn syrup
1 cup butter, no substitutes
1 (14 oz.) can sweetened
    condensed milk
1 tsp. vanilla extract

Butter an 8" square pan liberally; set aside.
Melt butter in a 3-quart saucepan, add sugar, corn syrup and the milk. Bring to a boil over medium heat, stirring constantly. Continue boiling on medium heat for 10 minutes while stirring constantly. Remove from heat; stir in vanilla.
Pour into prepared pan. Cool. Remove from pan and cut into 1/2"x1 1/2" rectangles. Wrap individually in pieces of waxed paper; twist ends.

Pecan Turtles

1 recipe creamy caramels,
    (see above)
1 1/4 - 1 1/2 lb. whole pecans

After stirring vanilla into caramel mixture, add the pecans and stir until well coated.
Drop by tablespoonful onto a greased and unlined baking sheet, about 1" apart. Chill until firm.

1 cup (6 oz.) semi-sweet
    chocolate chips
1 cup (6 oz.) milk chocolate
    chips
2 Tbsp. shortening

Melt chocolate with the shortening in microwave or double boiler. Drizzle over the turtles, or coat liberally according to taste. Chill until chocolate is firm.

-Marti

Peanut Clusters

6 oz. butterscotch morsels
12 oz. milk chocolate chips
12 oz. jar salted peanuts

Melt the butterscotch and chocolate morsels in a
microwave safe bowl or double boiler.
Add the jar of peanuts; mix until well coated.
Drop by teaspoonful onto a waxed paper lined hard
surface. Cool. Store in an airtight container.

Chocolate Covered Pretzels

pretzel twists
12 oz. semi-sweet chocolate chips
2 tsp. shortening
or
any color coating chocolate desired, such as red for
Valentines Day, etc.

Melt the chocolate chips and shortening in microwave or double
boiler. Remove from heat and dip pretzels; holding onto one side
of top rounded part of pretzel. Leave the area around your
fingers uncoated, exposing pretzel. Gently place onto a waxed
paper lined hard surface, and allow chocolate to harden.

Low
Sugar

LOW SUGAR

Peach Jello Mold

2 peaches, sliced, fresh or canned

Lightly oil the bottom and sides of an 8" or 9" round gelatin mold. Distribute the peach slices evenly in the bottom of mold.

2 (0.3 oz.) boxes sugar-free peach gelatin
2 cups boiling water
1 1/2 cups cold water

Pour the boiling water over the gelatin powder and stir until completely dissolved, about 1 - 2 minutes. Add the cold water and stir. Pour 1 cup of this mixture over the peaches.
Chill until set, about 1 hour. (Do not place remaining gelatin in refrigerator.)

2 cups 'lite' whipped topping

Mix a 3/4 cup of the gelatin with the whipped topping and whip until well blended. Spread this over the gelatin in mold and refrigerate for another 30 minutes.
Pour remaining gelatin over the whipped topping mixture and chill for 2 - 3 hours.
Just before serving, place jello mold in warm water for approximately 30 seconds before turning out onto serving tray.

Fill center with cottage cheese and/ or peach slices.

My thanks to Jason's aunt by marriage, Ann Raber, for sharing this recipe. Although her version was not sugar-free, we have enjoyed it this way for fewer calories.
-Carolyn

Sugar Free dressing for Potato Salad

2 cups mayonnaise
3 tsp. vinegar *or* lemon juice
1 tsp. salt
2 tsp. mustard
12 packets artificial sweetener
2 tsp. barbecue sauce

Combine all ingredients and mix thoroughly.

Makes 1 pint.

-Hannah

Low Sugar Pumpkin Chiffon Pie

8 oz. cream cheese

9 packets artificial sweetener, or more to taste

1 - 10" baked pie shells

3/4 cup cold milk
1 (1 oz.) box sugar-free instant vanilla pudding

1 (20 oz.) can pumpkin
2 tsp. allspice
1/2 cup lite whipped topping

'lite' whipped topping, optional

Beat cream cheese until light and fluffy.
Add the artificial sweetener, mixing on low speed just until blended.

Spread into bottom of pie shell.

In another bowl, combine pudding mix and milk and mix on low speed until combined. Beat on high speed for 2 minutes.
Add pumpkin, spice and whipped topping; mix on low speed just until well blended. Spread over cream cheese layer. Chill several hours or overnight. Top with whipped topping if desired.
Note: this is best if made a day ahead.

-Hannah

Sugar Free Apple Pie

2 cups water
3 1/2 Tbsp. clear jel

Place water and clear jel in a medium saucepan, mixing vigorously till clear jel is dissolved. Bring to a boil.

2 1/2 cups apples, sliced

Pour this mixture over the apples. Let cool.

1/2 cup Sugar Twin, (a brown sugar substitute
1/4 tsp. salt
1 1/2 tsp. cinnamon

Add next 3 ingredients and stir until well blended.

2 - 9" pie dough rounds, one pressed into a 9" plate, one reserved for top

Pour into the pie shell and cover with top shell. Crimp edges and slice through top crusts a few times for vents.

cinnamon
evaporated milk

Brush top of pies with evaporated milk and sprinkle with cinnamon. Bake at 350° for 40 - 45 minutes.

This is an extra good pie to make for diabetics. It is daddy's favorite dessert. So if I want to plan a special meal, I try to include this pie for him. (The way to a man's heart is through his stomach!)

-Mom

Sugar Free Strawberry Pie

2 1/2 cups water	*Place water in a small saucepan; bring to a boil.*
2 Tbsp. clear jel **4 Tbsp. water**	*Meanwhile combine the clear jel and water and add to the boiling mixture. Cook and stir until thick and clear, about 2 minutes. Remove from heat.*
1 small box sugar-free strawberry gelatin	*Add the gelatin.* *Cool for 1 hour.*
2 cups sliced strawberries	*Slice strawberries, reserving 6 of them for garnish. Pour slightly cooled filling over strawberries and stir.*
1 - 9" baked pie crust **1 (12 oz.) light whipped topping**	*Pour into crust and top with whipped topping and reserved strawberries for garnish.*

Use peach gelatin and fresh
peaches instead of strawberries for
a nice variation.

-Mom

Sugar Free Cake

1 cup prunes, pitted
1 cup dates, pitted
1 cup raisins
2 cups water

Combine the first 4 ingredients in a medium-sized saucepan and simmer until soft. Remove from heat. Cool.

1 cup oil
4 eggs
2 tsp. vanilla

Cream the next 3 ingredients together.

2 cups flour
2 tsp. soda
2 tsp. cinnamon

Fold in the dry ingredients.

1 cup chopped pecans

Add the stewed mixture and pecans and stir just until well blended. Pour into 2 loaf pans and bake at 325° for 45 minutes.

Sugar Free Raisin Pudding

1 small box instant sugar-free
  vanilla pudding
1 1/2 cups skim milk

Combine the pudding mix and milk according to directions. Let stand for 10 minutes.

1 cup raisins
1/2 tsp. vanilla
1 1/4 cup plain yogurt

Add raisins, vanilla and yogurt and mix until well blended.

whipped topping
cinnamon

Spoon into individual cups and top with the whipped topping and cinnamon if desired.

-Mom

Sour Cream Coffee Cake

1/4 cup margarine
1/4 cup brown sugar
Dry brown sugar substitute to
    equal 1/2 cup regular
    brown sugar
2 large eggs
1 cup sour cream
1 tsp. vanilla extract

2 cups all purpose flour
1/2 tsp. baking soda
1/2 tsp. baking powder
1/2 tsp. salt
1 tsp. cinnamon
1/4 cup water at room
    temperature

Cream these first 3 ingredients together at medium speed until light and fluffy.

Add the eggs, sour cream and vanilla and mix until creamy.

Combine the dry ingredients and add to the creamed mixture along with water, mixing well.

Spread batter into a greased 9" square baking pan.

Bake at 375° for 25 - 30 minutes, or until wooden pick inserted in center comes out clean.

Makes 16 servings.

-Mom

Raisin-Date Sugar Free Cookies

2 cups raisins
1 cup chopped dates
1 1/2 cups water

Place raisins, dates and water into a medium-sized saucepan and bring to a boil; boil for 5 minutes. Let cool.

4 eggs
3/4 Tbsp. vanilla extract
3/4 Tbsp. baking soda
1 cup margarine
3/4 tsp. cinnamon
1 3/4 cups flour

Cream eggs, margarine and vanilla. Add the cinnamon, flour and baking soda.

Combine this to the cooled fruit mixture; mix well.

Drop by teaspoonful onto baking sheets and bake at 350° for 8 - 10 minutes.

Makes 2 - 3 dozen.

-Kathleen

Equivalents

Ingredient	Quantity	Equivalent
apples, sliced	1 cup	1 large apple
baking powder	1 tsp.	1/4 tsp. soda + 1/2 tsp. cream of tarter
bananas, mashed	1 1/2 cups	3 medium bananas
berries	1 3/4 - 2 cups	1 pint
berries	3 1/2 - 4 cups	1 quart
bread crumbs	1 cup	2 slices
brown sugar	1 lb.	2 1/4 cups, firmly packed
buttermilk	1 cup	1 Tbsp. lemon juice + milk to equal 1 cup
cake flour	1 cup	1 cup minus 2 Tbsp. sifted all purpose
carrots	1 large	1 cup grated
celery stalks	2 medium	1 cup diced or chopped
cheddar cheese, shredded	1 cup	4 oz. cheese
chicken breast, boneless	1 whole	2 cups cooked
chocolate, unsweetened	1 oz.	3 Tbsp. cocoa + 1 Tbsp. butter
chocolate chips	1 cup	6 oz. package
corn starch	1 Tbsp.	2 Tbsp. all purpose flour
cream cheese	6 Tbsp.	3 oz. package
garlic	1 small clove	1/8 tsp. garlic powder, or minced garlic
graham cracker crumbs	1 cup	14 graham cracker squares
green pepper	1 large	1 cup diced
herbs, fresh, chopped	1 Tbsp.	1 tsp. dried
lemon	1 medium	2 - 3 Tbsp. freshly squeezed
milk, whole	1 cup	1/2 cup evaporated + 1/2 cup water
molasses	1 cup	1 cup honey
mustard, prepared	1 Tbsp	1 tsp. dry mustard + 2 tsp. vinegar
onion, chopped	1 small	1 Tbsp. minced dry onion
onion	1 medium	1/2 cup chopped
pecans, chopped	1 lb.	4 cups
potatoes	3 medium	1 3/4 cup mashed potatoes
powdered sugar	1 lb.	3 1/3 - 4 cups
self rising flour	1 cup	1 cup flour + 1 1/4 tsp. baking powder + 1/4 tsp. salt
sour cream	1 cup	3 Tbsp. butter + buttermilk or yogurt to equal 1 cup
sugar, granulated	1 lb.	2 cups
whipped cream	2 cups	1 cup heavy cream
wine, white	1/2 cup	1/2 cup apple or white grape juice
wine, red	1/2 cup	1/2 cup grape juice

General Index

In Pleasant Company
28938 River Road
Millington, Maryland 21651
410-810-3163

Please send me _____ copies of *Simply With Taste* at $15.95 per book. I am enclosing $2.50 for shipping and handling. Maryland residents please add $.80 per book for sales tax.

Name_____

Address_____

City_____State_____Zip_____

SAVE $1.00 on your order! Just send us the name and address of two gift or book stores in your area that sells cookbooks - and deduct $1.00 from your order.

Name of Store_____

Address_____

City_____State_____Zip_____

Name of Store_____

Address_____

City_____State_____Zip_____

- -

In Pleasant Company
28938 River Road
Millington, Maryland 21651
410-810-3163

Please send me _____ copies of *Simply With Taste* at $15.95 per book. I am enclosing $2.50 for shipping and handling. Maryland residents please add $.80 per book for sales tax.

Name_____

Address_____

City_____State_____Zip_____

SAVE $1.00 on your order! Just send us the name and address of two gift or book stores in your area that sells cookbooks - and deduct $1.00 from your order.

Name of Store_____

Address_____

City_____State_____Zip_____

Name of Store_____

Address_____

City_____State_____Zip_____